Trident
Britain's Independent Arms Race

Trident

Britain's Independent
Arms Race

Malcolm Chalmers

CND Publications Ltd

First published 1984 by
CND Publications Ltd.
Campaign for Nuclear Disarmament
11 Goodwin Street, London N4 3HQ

ISBN: 0 907321 11 9

Set by Red Lion Setters, Holborn, London.
Printed and bound in Great Britain by
Russell Press Ltd., Nottingham.

Contents

Acknowledgements

1. **Introduction**   1

2. **Britain and the Bomb**   4
   Britain's Bombs in the 1980s   5
   Theatre Nuclear Weapons   5
   The Strategic Force   9

3. **The Choice of Trident**   12
   Counterforce   12
   Only the Best for Britain   13
   A Major Escalation   14
   Whitehall Whitewash   19
   From the Grave   21
   Britain's First Strike Weapon   22
   'Decapitation'   25
   Launch on Warning?   26
   Is Trident Really Independent?   28
   Operational Independence   30

4. **Trident: What is it For?**   35
   Targeting Trident   35
   NATO's Second Centre   41
   The Sanctuary   42
   Britain Standing Alone   45
   Using Trident in the Third World   45
   1940 Revisited   47
   Nuclear Blackmail   49
   Britain's Nuclear Trigger   51
   The Real Reasons for Trident   52

5. **The Costs**   54
   The Coming Squeeze in Defence Spending   56
   A Cheaper Alternative?   58
   Trident Destroys Jobs   61

6. **Trident and Disarmament**   65
   Bombs for All   67
   Towards a Sensible Defence Policy   68

A Freeze Now   70
Conclusion   71

Notes   73

Guide to Further Reading   78

Glossary   79

Index   86

The Author

Malcolm Chalmers studied Economics at the Universities of Glasgow and Cambridge before working as an economist for the Government of Botswana. On his return, he moved to the University of East Anglia, where he obtained an MA in Development Economics, and began a study of the economics of British military spending. In 1982 he moved to the School of Peace Studies, University of Bradford, where he is now studying for a PhD on nuclear weapons and British defence policy. In 1983 he produced *The Cost of Britain's Defence*, which is published by the School of Peace Studies. A further book, entitled *Paying for Defence: Military spending and British decline* is due to be published by Pluto Press in April, 1985.

Malcolm has been a member of CND since 1975 and is also an active member of the Labour Party.

Acknowledgements

Thanks are due to Owen Greene and Paul Rogers for their helpful comments on a draft version. Adrian Howe and Denise Mooney of CND Publications and Meg Beresford of CND Publications Committee have been efficient, always encouraging, and patient. Deborah Robinson has been diligent in typing successive drafts of barely legible manuscripts.

Special thanks are due to Christine Halsall for her support and understanding, even when I should have been turning my attention to more important matters.

Chapter One

Introduction

In the last four years there has been a major change in public attitudes towards nuclear weapons. The strength of feeling has been demonstrated by the growth of a massive peace movement and by a vigorous public debate of issues previously the preserve of a few defence 'specialists'. Most significantly perhaps, the widespread dissatisfaction with current policy has been reflected in shifts in the positions of Britain's major political parties. As recently as 1980 there was a basic consensus on nuclear 'deterrence' between Labour and Tory leaders with the Labour defence spokesman, William Rodgers, still professing to be 'agnostic' on the question of Polaris replacement. Yet today, Labour leader Neil Kinnock's statement that he 'would never press the nuclear button', even in retaliation, appears to have been accepted by most of the Parliamentary Labour Party. The Liberal Party now has an official policy of opposition to Polaris and to cruise. Large sections of the Social Democratic and Conservative parties, while still hostile to 'unilateralism', now support a significant reduction in NATO's reliance on early use of nuclear weapons in a future conflict.

The isolation and unpopularity of the government on the nuclear issue is nowhere more evident than in its decision to proceed with the Trident programme. Public opinion polls show that only 28% of the population now support this decision,[1] and it is clear that the programme will be cancelled if Mrs Thatcher does not gain a clear majority at the next election. The armed forces, together with many Conservative MPs, are increasingly concerned at the effects which the £10 billion to be spent on Trident will have on Britain's conventional defences. This concern has been heightened by the Treasury's decision to allow little or no real growth in total defence spending from 1986 onwards. Indeed backbench scepticism is now such that, in the event of a genuinely free vote in Parliament, it must be doubtful whether Trident would survive – despite the large Conservative majority.

So far, however, the government has refused to respond to these pressures. It stubbornly defends Trident as a central element of its defence policy, and insists that it will contribute 'significantly to deterrence and hence the maintenance of peace.'[2] It continues to deny that it represents a massive escalation of the nuclear arms race which will reduce national security rather than increase it.

Yet, even in the world which military strategists inhabit, it is difficult to envisage any situation in which it would be rational to use this weapon. As Field Marshall Lord Carver has argued:

> Over the years the arguments have shifted and I have heard them all; but in that time I have never heard or read a scenario which I would consider to be realistic in which it could be considered to be right or reasonable for the Prime Minister or Government of this country to order the firing of our independent strategic force at a time when the Americans were not prepared to fire theirs – certainly not before Russian nuclear weapons had landed in this country. And, again, if they had already landed, would it be right and reasonable? All it would do would be to invite further retaliation.[3]

Indeed, it would be difficult to find a purely military explanation of the Trident decision. Rather it is a symbol of the Government's commitment to the illusion that Britain remains a Great Power. Nuclear weapons, it is believed, give Britain a higher status than the other middle ranking powers, albeit one still much below that of the two superpowers. The fact that the five permanent members of the United Nations Security Council – USA, USSR, France, Britain and China – are also the only acknowledged nuclear powers unfortunately adds weight to this contention.

Trident is, however, not simply a costly symbol of Britain's inability to adjust to the reality of economic decline. It is also an extremely dangerous development that will fuel the nuclear arms race and increase the risks of war. Contrary to government claims, it is not simply a 'replacement' for the current Polaris system. It is, instead, one of a new generation of highly accurate 'counterforce' nuclear weapons which encourage the illusion that nuclear wars can be fought and won, and threaten to put the arsenals of both superpowers on a hairtrigger.

Moreover, Trident will further complicate the prospects for arms talks between the two superpowers: the Soviet Union is likely to insist on having as many warheads as NATO as a whole, including the UK. Yet the United States is unlikely to accept any deal which permits it to have less weapons than the Soviets. As long as the arsenals of Britain and France are relatively small, this problem may be manageable. But if Britain expands the number of targets its strategic nuclear force can hit by a factor of between 8 and 14 – as Trident would do – the prospects for strategic arms limitation will diminish still further.

Finally, Trident is likely to encourage the spread of nuclear weapons. Britain is a country in a relatively peaceful region of the world, with no immediate threat to its national security, yet it feels a need to build up the size of its nuclear forces. It cannot, therefore, be very convincing in persuading states in much less stable areas – such as Israel, Pakistan and Iraq – not to acquire a nuclear force of their own. Yet if nuclear weapons spread to 10, 15 or 20 countries – as is possible over the next two decades – the chances of putting the nuclear genie back in its bottle will diminish still further. The possibility of a limited nuclear conflict in the Third World will, sooner or later, become a reality, and could trigger a global holocaust.

Stop Trident

For all these reasons, therefore, the need to stop Trident is urgent. It encourages dangerous ideas of 'nuclear warfighting', it complicates the prospects for superpower arms talks, and it encourages non-nuclear states to acquire their own nuclear forces. Cancellation could, on the other hand, be a significant contribution in reducing the risks of nuclear war, and thus in increasing British security. It could help to break the current build-up of tension between the two blocs, and thus facilitate a climate in which further disarmament is possible. By cancelling Trident, Britain could start the process of political and military re-thinking that will be necessary if genuine multilateral disarmament is to be achieved.

Such a move will not be easy, questioning as it does the outmoded ideas of national power still held by many of our leaders. Yet it is a move that is clearly necessary. Ever since 1945, humanity has been living on borrowed time. The development of new technologies, the increase in Cold War rhetoric, and the militarisation of the Third World all suggest that the possibilities of nuclear war are not decreasing. If this opportunity is lost, we may not have another chance. This book, I hope, will help provide some of the information that campaigners will need if they are to win the argument against Trident – and take a first step towards securing all our futures.

Chapter Two
Britain and the Bomb

Throughout the period since World War Two, British governments – Labour and Conservative – have attempted to compensate for economic decline by an obsession with military strength. As a result Britain has consistently spent a greater proportion of its national income on defence than most of its industrial competitors, and relative economic decline has accelerated further. The decision to become a nuclear power was a direct consequence of this obsession.

In the 1940s Britain's leaders at this time still saw their country – or more accurately their Empire – as a Great Power. They had, after all, just emerged victorious from world-war, and had been one of the big Three at the summits in Yalta and Potsdam who determined the division of the postwar world into spheres of influence. The secret decisions in 1946 and 1947 to develop a British atomic bomb were a direct result of this perception. Without it, Britain would 'sink to the rank of a second class nation', as one senior official put it.[1]

Even at this stage, however, there was important opposition to the project from the more farsighted within the government. One of the government's most senior advisors, Patrick Blackett, argued in a confidential memorandum that:

> It is probable that the decision to manufacture or to acquire atomic bombs now would tend to decrease rather than to increase our long-term security...[2]

Two years later, in 1949, the government chief scientist, Henry Tizard, came out against the project and wrote:

> We persist in regarding ourselves as a Great Power, capable of everything and only temporarily handicapped by economic difficulties. We are not a Great Power and never will be again... if we continue to behave like a Great Power we shall soon cease to be a great nation.[3]

Indeed by 1949 the costs of the A-bomb project were becoming so great that the military Chiefs of Staff requested that it be given a lower priority in order to release resources for other weapons.[4]

These objections in private were not to carry weight. In 1952,

Britain's nuclear programme was given top priority by Winston Churchill's Government with the decision to approve the 'Global Strategy Paper'. This paper argued that Britain could remain a Great Power only by relying on nuclear weapons. Its acceptance by Britain was influential in persuading the American government to move towards a policy of 'massive retaliation'; as a consequence, tactical nuclear weapons were rapidly integrated into every branch of NATO armed forces in the mid and late 1950s.[5]

The Global Strategy Paper led to an increased emphasis being placed on Britain's 'independent deterrent' – first the V-bombers and then the Polaris submarines. Throughout the 1950s and 1960s, the possession of these weapons was used as part of an attempt to deny the decline in Britain's world position. After the humilating defeat of Britain's diplomacy at Suez in 1956, it enabled the new Prime Minister, Harold Macmillan, to claim:

> The independent (nuclear force)...gives us a better position in the world, it gives us a better position with respect to the United States. It puts us where we ought to be, in the position of a Great Power.[6]

Even Nye Bevan, standard bearer of Labour's left wing, revised his earlier unilateralist views and argued that a renunciation of the nuclear force would 'send a British Foreign Secretary, whoever he may be, naked into the conference chamber.'[7]

Britain's Bombs in the 1980s

As a result of the high priority attached to nuclear weapons over several decades, Britain now has a wide range of nuclear weapons. It is unclear exactly how many. Estimates vary from 577 to 1500.[8] Though we do not know precisely how many bombs Britain possesses, we do know which weapon systems are designed to carry them – the so-called 'nuclear capable systems'. (See box, pages 6-7.)

Britain's nuclear forces fall into two categories – theatre forces and strategic forces. Though these are by no means water-tight categories, they do help us to understand the distinct functions of different weapons.

Theatre Nuclear Weapons

Most of Britain's nuclear-capable systems are *theatre nuclear weapons*. These are weapons designed for use in a limited nuclear

Britain's Nuclear Arsenal

Polaris

Britain's strategic nuclear force. Consists of four submarines, each equipped with sixteen missiles. Each missile has a range of 2500 miles, and carries three 200 kiloton warheads. The front end of the missile is currently being updated with the Chevaline system (see text for more details).

Battlefield Nuclear Weapons

The British Army of the Rhine, based in West Germany, has a number of systems designed for use in a limited nuclear war. These include 138 M109 and M110 howitzers and 12 Lance missile launchers. Each is capable of launching several nuclear weapons in succession. The M109, for example, can launch nuclear shells at the rate of one per minute.

At present these systems are designed to take American warheads—on a 'dual-key' arrangement—with yields of from less than 1 kiloton to 100 kilotons. In future, they could be equipped with US enhanced radiation warheads (or 'neutron bombs').

Nuclear-Capable Aircraft

The Royal Air Force currently has 18 squadrons of nuclear-capable aircraft. These include 72 Jaguars based at Coltishall, Norfolk and Bruggen, West Germany; 36 Nimrods at St Mawgan, Cornwall and Kinloss, Morayshire; 32 Buccaneers at Lossiemouth, Morayshire; and a growing number, well over 100 to date, of Tornadoes based so far at Marham, Norfolk and Laarback, West Germany. In the mid-1980s, these will be supplemented by 100 more Tornadoes and 62 nuclear-capable Harrier GR5 aircraft.

The Nimrods are equipped to carry a US nuclear depth bomb with a yield of between 1 kiloton and 20 kilotons. Other

nuclear-capable aircraft are equipped with British made nuclear weapons. The Tornadoes (above) and possibly the Buccaneers will carry a 'medium-weight' warhead, probably with a variable yield of up to 500 kilotons. Other aircraft—the Jaguar, Harrier GR5, and Buccaneer—carry a 'light-weight' warhead with a maximum yield of around 20 kilotons.

Nuclear Weapons for War at Sea

Most of the Royal Navy's major surface ships—carriers, destroyers, and frigates—carry nuclear-capable helicopters. These are equipped to carry British-made nuclear depth bombs for use in naval nuclear warfare. Each bomb is thought to have a yield of less than 20 kilotons. The Navy's nuclear-capable helicopters currently include 64 Sea Kings (each able to carry four nuclear depth bombs), 23 Wasps, and 66 Lynx. The new EH101 helicopter, now under development, will also be nuclear-capable. Whilst most ships do not carry nuclear weapons for their helicopters at all times, it is likely that the largest ships—such as the Invincible-class carriers—carry nuclear warheads routinely.

The Royal Navy's carriers are also equipped with 24 Sea Harrier aircraft, which can deliver British-made freefall tactical nuclear bombs with a yield of around 15 kilotons. These are for use against other surface ships, and possibly against targets on land. A further 14 Sea Harriers are on order.

Note: I am grateful to Paul Rogers for permission to reproduce this information, which is based on his Guide to Nuclear Weapons, 1984-85 (Bradford, School of Peace Studies, 1984).

war – one that is limited to a particular 'theatre' of conflict such as
Europe. They form an important part of NATO's policy of
'flexible response', which provides for the First Use of nuclear
weapons against a non-nuclear Soviet attack should NATO be
seen to be losing. Because of the Soviet Union's own nuclear
bombs, it is thought that a threat to destroy its cities in retaliation
for a conventional attack – the 'massive retaliation' policy of the
1950s – would not be 'credible'. Instead, therefore, a more limited
nuclear response is planned – a 'flexible' response.

NATO's policy of flexible response, and in particular the reliance
on short range 'battlefield' nuclear weapons, is now coming under
heavy criticism from both inside and outside the military. Theatre
nuclear weapons are now so closely integrated into the armed forces
of NATO members that they would be used long before conventional defence could even be given a chance to work. Indeed, one
leading American strategic studies specialist has argued that this
integration is a deliberate consequence of government policy:

> The NATO strategy of relying on nuclear weapons is politically
> and militarily credible because the governing command structure is
> so unstable and accident-prone that national leaders would exercise
> little practical control over it in wartime. What other command
> mechanisms could possibly be built to invoke a nuclear conflict
> that, for all practical purposes, is tantamount to a regional dooms-
> day machine?[9]

Critics of current policy are opposed to indefinite reliance on this
'doomsday machine' for their survival. They argue that it would, at
the very least, be very difficult to prevent a conflict escalating rapidly
to a global holocaust once more than a handful of 'battlefield' nukes
are exchanged. Even if war could be limited geographically, the
'theatre' of operations, (Europe), would be utterly devastated.

As a consequence of arguments such as these, there is now a
large body of opinion that believes that NATO should move
rapidly towards a policy of No First Use of nuclear weapons. Such
a policy would permit the scrapping of most if not all of the existing arsenal of theatre weapons – including Britain's nuclear artillery, depth charges, and freefall bombs. It would leave nuclear
weapons with no military purpose beyond deterring their use by
the other side – a function for which only a relatively small
'minimum deterrent' would be required.

Arguments for No First Use and minimum deterrence, however, have been rejected out of hand by all three Western nuclear
powers. Like the US and France, Britain continues to modernise

and 'improve' its own battlefield nuclear weapons. The introduction of Tornado nuclear bombers, together with Harrier GR5 aircraft, will represent a major expansion of the Royal Air Force's nuclear strike power. Already, in 1983, the number of nuclear capable howitzers with the British Army on the Rhine has been expanded from 66 to 135.[10] Also, the possibility of a future British cruise missile force, for use in limited wars, still appears to be a very real one.

The Strategic Force

For our purposes in this volume, however, the most important part of Britain's present nuclear arsenal is its four *Polaris* submarines. Each of these submarines is capable of launching 16 missiles at targets deep inside the Soviet Union; each missile carries 3 warheads, probably of 200 kilotons each. Used against a 'soft' target – such as a city – a Polaris missile would have a destructive power, with these warheads, of around 48 times that of the bomb that destroyed Hiroshima.

It is the capability to destroy targets within the Soviet Union, and the intention to use it to do so, that makes Polaris the main 'strategic' nuclear weapon in Britain's possession. It is this role which, it is planned, Trident will take on when Polaris is phased out in the 1990s.

Britain's Polaris force, was and is, heavily dependent on the supply of key components and technology from the United States. The 1962 Nassau agreement provided that the US would supply Polaris missiles to Britain, while Britain would build its own submarines and nuclear warheads. In return, Prime Minister Macmillan agreed that Polaris 'will be used for the purposes of international defence of the Western Alliance in all circumstances' except 'where Her Majesty's Government may decide that supreme national interests are at stake.'[12]

Since it is inconceivable that Polaris will be used *unless* Britain believes its 'supreme national interests' are at stake, the real meaning of this latter commitment remains a matter of speculation. In practice its main effect is to enable British governments to describe Polaris as either an 'independent deterrent' or as a 'contribution to NATO' according to what was most politically convenient at the time. Conservative governments usually prefer to emphasise the independent role of Polaris, seeking to represent it as a symbol of Britain's continued world status. Labour governments, on the other hand, have played down the independent role. In deference to the strong anti-nuclear wing of their own party, their public pronouncements have concentrated on the 'contribution to NATO' aspect of Polaris.

The difference between the two parties in government, however, has so far been more one of presentation than of policy. In reality Labour leaders appear to have been as eager as Conservatives to retain a British nuclear force. The contrast between the secretive decision-making under the Wilson and Callaghan administrations, and the more open approach under Mrs Thatcher, reflects the different political pressures to which leaders of the major parties are subject – their basic aims have been remarkably similar.

The political convergence between Labour and Conservative was clearly demonstrated in the *Chevaline* programme to update Britain's Polaris missiles. The project started development under Edward Heath in 1973, was retained by Labour through its 1975 defence review, and was completed under Mrs Thatcher in 1983-4. Despite being the most important development in Britain's nuclear force for a decade, it was not until 1980 that the House of Commons was told of its existence. By then it was nearing completion.

The need for *Chevaline* was first suggested in the 1960s. Both superpowers had ambitious plans for Anti-Ballistic Missile (ABM) defences, which would enable them, it was hoped, to shoot down incoming enemy missiles. British planners feared that, on a 'worst case' analysis of possible Soviet defences, they might lose the capability to destroy Moscow. This requirement – the 'Moscow criterion' – was widely held to be a necessary part of remaining a fully fledged nuclear power. *Chevaline*, at least initially, was largely a result of commitment to the 'Moscow criterion'.

Chevaline is a complex system designed to evade and confuse Soviet missile defences. It uses both a manoeuvrable space craft and an unspecified number of decoy warheads for this purpose. Its total cost, based on government figures, comes to around £2,200 million in 1984 prices – almost as much as the £2,300 million spent on the original Polaris programme itself.[13]

Despite this massive expenditure, however, *Chevaline* has proven to be of little or no military value, even in the questionable dreamworld of nuclear planners. The 1972 ABM Treaty between the two superpowers had curtailed the deployment of missile defences around Moscow, more in recognition of the technical difficulties involved than as a result of a genuine commitment to curbing the arms race. As a result, Britain's Polaris missiles would have been capable of destroying Moscow into the foreseeable future even without the *Chevaline* update.

Partly as a result of the ABM Treaty, and partly because of the worsening economic situation, *Chevaline* was subject to a major review in 1974 and 1975. It survived untouched, not so much, it seems, because of the 'Moscow criterion' as because of the desire to keep Britain's team of nuclear warhead experts together. As Lawrence Freedman argues:

> (If *Chevaline*) was to be abandoned with nothing else in the offing until the 1980s, then it would prove difficult to maintain morale in the laboratories and keep together a qualified design team until such time as it could be properly employed . . . Cancellation would be taken as a major turning point in British nuclear weapons policy, as an indication of being prepared to wind down the whole force. This was not the Government's intention and so the line of least resistance was to let the programme run its course.[14]

Despite Labour's 1974 Manifesto commitment not 'to move towards the production of a new generation of strategic nuclear weapons', a primary consideration in the *Chevaline* decision was undoubtedly the desire to retain the option to replace Polaris entirely in the 1990s. Indeed, as the next chapter points out, the Labour Government would almost certainly have decided to break that commitment had it not been defeated in the 1979 General Election.

Chapter Three
The Choice of Trident

By the early 1990s the existing Polaris submarines will be nearing the end of their useful life, and will become increasingly unreliable. Spare parts, servicing and fuel for the Polaris missiles will become increasingly expensive as US sources of supply dry up and stocks are exhausted. The last United States Polaris missile has now been withdrawn from service: the cost of maintaining Polaris facilities for British-only use is bound to increase.

In the late 1970s, as a result of these factors, military experts argued that, if the government wished to retain a British strategic nuclear force after 1993, (or thereabouts), it would need to decide how it wished to replace the Polaris force. It would also need to make a decision soon if there was to be enough time to develop and build this replacement.

In 1977, acting upon this advice, the Labour government set up a committee to study the matter. Its members were Prime Minister James Callaghan, Denis Healey (then Chancellor of the Exchequer), David Owen (Foreign Secretary), and Fred Mulley (Defence Secretary). Its deliberations were kept secret even from other members of the Cabinet. By early 1979 its discussions were far enough advanced for Mr Callaghan to raise the possibility of American help in discussions with President Carter at the Guadalope summit.

The final decision to purchase Trident was not, however, taken under Labour. It was left to the Conservatives, elected in May 1979, to do that. But the extensive studies prepared under Mr Callaghan meant that the Conservative's own secret Cabinet subcommittee (Thatcher, Whitelaw, Howe, Pym, Carrington) was able to move rapidly to a decision. That decision – made public in July 1980 – was to purchase the US Trident C4 system. As with Polaris, the submarines and warheads would be made in Britain, while the missile would be supplied by the Americans. The total cost of the project was estimated to be between £4,500 million and £5,000 million (at September 1980 prices) – more than two and a half times that of the original Polaris programme after allowing for inflation.[1]

Counterforce

While Britain was deciding on its Polaris replacement, nuclear policy on the other side of the Atlantic was also undergoing significant development. Increasing emphasis was being given to the need for nuclear weapons that were accurate enough to destroy Soviet nuclear missiles in hardened silos. This capability, it was argued, was necessary to give the United States the capability to fight, and in some sense 'win', a nuclear war. The move towards 'counterforce' and warwinning strategies had been developing under President Carter. Under President Reagan, however, it gained a new impetus. One of the most important consequences of the shift in US policy was the decision, announced in October 1981, to develop and produce a completely new submarine-launched ballistic missile (SLBM) – *Trident D5*.[2] By the 1990s, it is planned, Trident D5 will be the largest single component of the United States strategic nuclear arsenal. It will give the United States the capability of destroying almost all Soviet landbased nuclear weapons missiles (ICBMs) in a 'disarming first strike': a capability which threatens to add a new, and dangerous twist to the superpower arms race.

Only the Best for Britain

In March 1982, shortly after the US decision to develop the D5 missile, Britain followed suit, justifying its shift by the need to retain 'commonality' with the Americans. This decision was as significant as the initial one to opt for C4. For, despite the similarity in names, the D5 is in reality a completely new, and much more dangerous, weapon.

Britain's decision to buy the D5 missile – still unproven in the USA – was only one example of a tendency to go for the most sophisticated, and therefore usually the most expensive, technologies available. It was also seen in the simultaneous decisions to purchase new and untested systems for Trident's tactical weapon systems – those for protection against Soviet submarines – and in the adoption of a new reactor and propulsion system – the Pressurised Water Reactor Mark Two (PWR2). Far from it being a minimum deterrent, Trident is a case of maximum hedging. As a result of the more sophisticated missile, together with these other improvements, the estimated total cost of Britain's Trident project rose to £7,500 million (at September 1981 prices).[3]

Because of the government's determination to get the 'best' system available, and to insure against any possible countermeasures into the 2020s, Trident will not simply be a replacement for the ageing Polaris force. Rather, it will be a major expansion in

Britain's nuclear weapon force which will be directly contrary to the stated government commitment to balanced (or 'multilateral') disarmament. Trident will (i) be a massive *quantitative* expansion in Britain's nuclear force and (ii) mark a dangerous *qualitative* change in the type of targets which Britain can attack.

A Major Escalation

Trident will have many more warheads than the Polaris/*Chevaline* system it replaces; it will be able to destroy a much larger number of separate targets. It thus represents a massive quantitative expansion in Britain's strategic nuclear firepower.

Before the *Chevaline* update, there were three 200 kiloton warheads on each Polaris missile. It is probable that there are still three warheads per missile, but with the addition of a number of decoys or 'dummy' warheads. However, although each missile has three warheads, it can only be used against a single target. The purpose of its multiple warhead system (called MRV for short) is to confuse and overwhelm Anti-Ballistic missile defences (ABMs), and to achieve maximum destructive effect. MRV warheads cannot be used on separate targets: they spread like buckshot over a specified area up to, perhaps, 10 miles apart.

Trident, by contrast, will have Multiple Independently Targetable Re-entry Vehicles (MIRVs for short). These will be supplied by the US as part of the agreement between President Reagan and Mrs Thatcher, and will allow each warhead to be aimed independently, greatly increasing the total number of targets that can be destroyed.

Each of the Trident D5 missiles will be able to carry up to 17 warheads. The provisions of the unratified SALT II Treaty, however, only allow a maximum of 14 warheads to be deployed on each MIRVed submarine launched missile, and the US has so far agreed to abide by this provision. The indications are that Britain will follow the US lead.

Considerable uncertainty remains, however, as to the exact number of warheads which will eventually be deployed on Trident. The theoretical maximum is 896: 4 submarines with 16 missiles each and 14 warheads per missile. But the government does not appear to have made a final decision on this question. In 1982 the Secretary of State for Defence, John Nott, stated that:

> Our plans *at the moment* do not envisage a greater number of warheads in total than we were contemplating putting on C4[4] (ie, 512 warheads). (Author's emphasis.)

Figure 1:
Trident: A Cost Breakdown

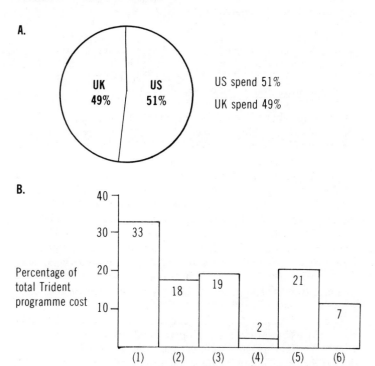

A.

UK 49% US 51%

US spend 51%

UK spend 49%

B.

Percentage of total Trident programme cost

33 (1) 18 (2) 19 (3) 2 (4) 21 (5) 7 (6)

1. Submarines (excluding weapon system equipment)
2. Weapon system equipment (including tactical systems)
3. Nuclear missiles
4. Shore construction
5. Warheads, miscellaneous, unallocated contingency.
6. Other

Source: Author's own estimates. See Chapter 5 for further discussion.

Notes: (i) based on September 1984 prices and on exchange rate of £1 = $1.40.

(ii) 'Other' includes funds for new facilities at Aldermaston and Vickers.

(iii) Categories used are derived from The United Kingdom Trident Programme, Defence Open Document 82/1 (London HMSO, 1982), p.7.

(iv) 'Weapon system equipment' indicates systems used to defend the Trident submarines from attack—sonar, torpedoes, etc. It does not include the nuclear missiles themselves.

Given the low financial cost of deploying additional warheads, however, it is possible that military planners will not adhere rigidly to the artificial ceiling of 512. As John Nott himself conceded in the same statement:

> The system will not come into service until the mid-1990s but my successors and the Prime Minister at the time would have complete choice as to how many missiles were placed in the submarine, and similarly the Prime Minister at the time would have a choice as to the number of warheads that were placed on that missile.[5]

The total number of warheads on Britain's Trident missiles, therefore, could be anything between 512 and 896. Trident will therefore be able to destroy between 8 and 14 times as many different targets as the present Polaris/*Chevaline* force (see Figure 2).

Like the planned number of warheads, the *explosive power* of Trident's warheads is a closely guarded secret. The US Navy's 6,000 D5 warheads will each have a yield of up to 475 kilotons.[6] Britain's warheads, however, are designed and built independently. They will probably have a smaller yield than the US warheads – the best current estimate is 100 kilotons.[7] If this estimate proves to be correct, the UK's four Trident submarines will have a total explosive force of up to 90 megatons – more than twice as much as that of the current Polaris force, and *equivalent to 7200 Hiroshima bombs*.

The escalation which Trident represents will be further increased by its much greater operational *availability*. The new PWR2 nuclear reactor, which will power the submarine, is designed to have a much longer reactor core life. The D5 missiles can be serviced – unlike Polaris – without removing them from their launch tubes. As a result, the need for major refits will be rediced, and the availability of the submarines for patrol greatly increased. Due to the requirements for repairs and refits, only two of the four Polaris boats are on patrol for 73% of the time, whilst for 20% of the year only one boat is available.[8] Trident, by contrast, will have three submarines available for over 80 per cent of the time.[9]

As a direct consequence of this increased availability, the number of targets that Britain is likely to be able to destroy will increase by an even greater factor than the number of warheads suggests. The present Polaris fleet is only able to destroy either 16 or 32 targets, depending on how many boats are available. Trident will be able to destroy up to either 448 or 672. Trident will therefore in practice be able to destroy between 21 and 28 times as many targets as Polaris can at present – a quite remarkable increase for a weapon described as a 'replacement system'.

Trident will also be able to target a much larger area than Polaris. It will have a *range* of 6,000 miles, compared with Polaris's 2,500 miles. It will be able to cover the whole Soviet Union, not simply that portion West of the Urals as at present, from patrol in the Eastern Atlantic. It will, if required, be able to target other continents too (see Figure 3). Combined with the considerable increase in warhead numbers, Trident's range will give Britain a capacity for destroying every large and medium-sized city in the Soviet Union. The eastern Soviet republics will no longer be exempt from the British bomb. Other actual or potential nuclear powers – China, Japan, India, South Korea – will fall within range of Britain's missiles for the first time.

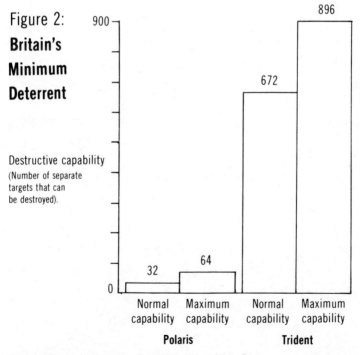

Figure 2:
Britain's Minimum Deterrent

Destructive capability
(Number of separate targets that can be destroyed).

Note: See text for detailed explanation and discussion of these figures.

* According to Michael Heseltine, 'The Trident force will be the minimum size necessary to provide a credible and effective deterrent'. (House of Commons June 18, 1984, col. 40.)

Figure 3:
Trident's increased range

Trident also makes 'limited nuclear war' an apparently more plausible proposition. At present the firing of a single missile is liable to reveal the location of a Polaris submarine, and since the missile's limited range restricts its patrol area, this then makes the submarine vulnerable to destruction by Soviet ASW forces. With only one, or at most two submarines on patrol, there is therefore a severe constraint on using Polaris for controlled nuclear escalation. By its technical nature, Polaris is suited only to an all-out nuclear 'countercity' role.

Trident, by contrast, will have a much greater capability for limited nuclear war. Its increased range means that it is much more likely to be able to escape destruction after the firing of a single missile. The increased availability of submarines on patrol means that the loss of one submarine would not destroy Britain's 'last resort deterrent', and its increased accuracy threatens a much larger variety of hardened, military targets.

Indeed, the planned accuracy of its warheads is perhaps the most dangerous aspect of Trident. The current Polaris/*Chevaline* force can only be used against large, or unprotected, 'soft' targets – such as cities. Trident D5, on the other hand, will be accurate enough to destroy hardened military targets such as missile silos and command bunkers: a crucial requirement in the US programme to acquire a 'first strike' capability.

By purchasing re-entry vehicles from the United States, Britain's Trident missiles will also be able to achieve a high level of accuracy. This capability is quite superfluous if the sole purpose of Trident (for the UK) is retaliation for a Soviet nuclear attack. It is only of use in destroying an enemy's nuclear weapons *before* they are fired. It implicates Britain very directly in the plans for nuclear warfighting and counterforce, which provide the impetus for President Reagan's nuclear arms build-up. Britain's acquisition of Trident D5 thus represents a major *qualitative* escalation in its nuclear capability.

Whitehall Whitewash

According to the government, however, Trident is no more than is needed as a 'replacement' of the existing Polaris fleet, and can therefore not be described as an escalation in Britain's nuclear force. It justifies this contention by arguing that three of Trident's new features – its greater number of warheads, its increased availability, and its longer range – are no more than is needed to keep pace with possible improvements in Soviet defences, and thus to ensure the continued credibility of Britain's 'minimum deterrent.' It also contends that Trident's silo-killing accuracy played no part in the decision to acquire it. Britain's Trident force alone, it claims, would be too small for use in a 'disarming first strike'.

The rest of this chapter will examine these arguments in detail. For they demonstrate powerfully the way in which the nuclear arms race has developed a momentum of its own. They also show that our government's narrow concept of national security threatens to further destabilise an already precarious balance of terror.

The contention that Trident just replaces Polaris as a 'weapon of last resort', rests on the need to guarantee that its missiles, once fired, will *penetrate* Soviet defences and destroy the targets – at present major cities – for which they are intended. Trident's nuclear weapons should in turn *survive* a surprise Soviet attack. These two criteria – 'penetrability' and 'survivability' – are the basis on which the government has constructed its defence of the Trident project.

Yet these arguments, even on their own terms, are remarkably weak. In the two main areas of technological development which could threaten the nuclear force's effectiveness – Anti-Ballistic Missile Defences (ABM) and strategic Anti-Submarine Warfare (ASW) – the Soviet Union's present capability is very poor. It is only by making a series of extremely pessimistic – or 'worst-case' – assumptions of long term developments in these two fields that the Government is able to 'justify' the massive quantitative escalation which Trident involves.

For example, the government justifies the need for MIRVing the warheads on Trident by the requirement to overcome Soviet anti-ballistic missile (ABM) defences – in particular those around Moscow. It argues that for its deterrent to be 'credible', Britain must be able to ensure the destruction of the Soviet capital, which contains most of the Soviet elite and whose loss would be a crippling blow to the Soviet state. By increasing the number of warheads arriving simultaneously on different flight paths, Trident will be able to overwhelm any ABM defences which the Soviets can develop. This argument encounters the difficulty that current Soviet ABM defences – the Galosh system – are primitive, and likely to be ineffective even against a direct Polaris attack on Moscow.

The Government also assumes that the current ABM Treaty between the Soviet Union and the US, which limits the Soviet

Union to a maximum of 100 launchers around Moscow, will be abandoned. This may not be an unreasonable assumption, given the massive programmes of research and development (R&D), by both superpowers, of systems which, if deployed, would breach this treaty. Secondly, it assumes that the Soviets will follow the US quest for effective 'star wars' defences against ballistic missiles. Thirdly, and most problematically, it assumes that the massive amounts being spent on these new technologies will actually succeed in meeting their ambitious objectives. If the Government then projects President Reagan's dreams of 'making the world safe again' to the year 2020, and assumes that the Soviets can, more or less, keep pace with US developments (both highly questionable assumptions), then the case for sophisticated MIRVed warheads is made. For otherwise, by the year 2020, the Soviets *might* be able to destroy British missiles on their way to Moscow. And, it is argued, Britain does not simply have to pose some *risk* of its missiles getting through. It needs to ensure a *near certainty* if 'deterrence' is to be preserved.

Trident, therefore, is not a response to existing Soviet defences, or even to those likely in the 1990s. Instead it is designed to counter possible technological developments over the next 30 or 40 years, on the pessimistic assumption that they will not be significantly constrained by arms control agreements. This time period is as great as that between the late 1930s and the present day, and may well see as profound a process of technical change. It is perhaps inevitable that cautious military planners will assume the worst in their scenarios for the 2020s. It is unfortunate that they do not pay as much attention to considering our chances of surviving until that distant decade if the arms race continues unbridled.

From the Grave

The second criterion, 'survivability', uses the same type of 'worst case' analysis to justify Trident's increased *range* and *availability*. At present submarine-launched missiles are the least vulnerable part of Western nuclear forces in the event of a surprise attack. Landbased missiles (cruise, MX, Minuteman), bombers (Tornado, F111, B52), and submarines in port would all be targets in a large scale disarming first strike. Submarines at sea, however, could escape such an attack and still be able to retaliate 'from the grave'.

Indeed, the invulnerability of submarine-based missiles is seen as their major attraction. It will ensure that, even if the entire country were devastated in a surprise attack, revenge would be possible. For this purpose Britain's Polaris submarine commanders apparently are able to fire their missiles without any political authorisation if they believe that 'no responsible person is in a position to transmit orders to them.'[10]

In the distant future, however, it is possible that the Soviets will develop Anti-Submarine Warfare (ASW) capabilities that make the seas more 'transparent', and allow them to destroy enemy submarines as part of a first strike. By ensuring more submarines are on patrol at any one time, Trident will counter Soviet advances in both ASW and ABM defences. More British submarines will have to be destroyed over a short period of time, and more missiles will be available to penetrate the defences round Moscow.

More important, Trident's enormously increased range means that it will be able to patrol much further away from its potential targets. The submarines will thus be more difficult to track for Soviet forces – submarines, aircraft, and surface ships – assigned to submarine hunting. Indeed, Trident's range would enable Britain to deploy submarines virtually anywhere in the world – out of reach of the Soviet Navy but still within range of Soviet cities. One author suggested that:

> If Britain and France could put submarines into the Indian Ocean, even for a limited period, the Soviet Union would be hard pressed to threaten them in any effective first-strike mode unless it were prepared to deploy a permanent ASW flotilla in that vast area.[11]

Yet, according to government evidence, no British Polaris submarine has ever been found on patrol by the Soviet Navy.[12] Only by 'worst case' technical projections into the first decade of the next century and beyond can the preparations involved in Trident possibly be justified. Such a procedure is a recipe both for further dangerous escalation and for exorbitant expense.

Britain's First Strike Weapon

While its increased range and availability were acknowledged factors in the decision to opt for Trident D5 rather than possible alternatives, the government has denied that its silo-killing accuracy was considered to be relevant. 'Defence Open Government Document 82/1', which explains the decision in detail, states:

The Government wishes to make it absolutely clear that the increased accuracy of the Trident D5 system played no part in its decision to adopt the more modern system.[13]

It points out that:

even if a UK Government had any thoughts of a first strike capability, simple arithmetic demonstrates that it is totally beyond its grasp. The firepower of the British force with maximum D5 payloads would be sufficient to target only a very small proportion of the Soviet ICBM silos.

To forestall the observant reader who may be asking himself or herself whether this implies that the US is seeking a first strike capability by acquiring 6,000 D5 warheads, it continues:

the reasons behind the UK and US decisions to deploy D5 are very different ... The purpose of the US ... is to make it clear that it has the ability to use its nuclear weapons ... against different numbers and types of targets including specifically military targets. This is made possible by the increased accuracy of the more modern missile. Their policy ... is not in any way to provide a 'first strike' capability or to make 'limited nuclear war' easier or more likely; neither the US, the UK nor NATO as a whole subscribes to either concept.

These statements are quite untenable. It is indeed difficult to tell how the government has felt able to make them. The contention that Trident's increased accuracy is unrelated to US plans for a limited nuclear war and for a first strike capability, yet is designed for use against hardened military targets, will strike most people as pure sophistry. The entire basis of recent American nuclear planning has been precisely to provide the President with a range of 'limited nuclear options' for the conduct of a 'protracted nuclear war'. The statement that British decisionmakers were entirely uninterested in Trident's increased accuracy has been greeted with some scepticism in Britain, and is no doubt viewed with derision in the Soviet Union. For it is clearly inconsistent with its integration into US strategic nuclear targeting plans (see p. 24).

Such scepticism is likely to be reinforced by the contention that the maximum payload on the British Trident force could target 'only a very small proportion of the Soviet ICBM silos'. The maximum payload which Britain could deploy in four 16-tube submarines will be 896 highly accurate D5 warheads. At present the Soviet Union has 1378 ICBMs (Intercontinental Ballistic

Trident and Counterforce

The most dangerous technological trend in the nuclear arms race at present is undoubtedly the rapid improvement in the accuracy of nuclear missiles. Highly accurate weapons enable one side to destroy the other's missile silos and command bunkers before they can be used in retaliation. Were one side then to believe that it had the capability to destroy all, or almost all, the opponent's nuclear forces in a 'disarming first strike', the incentives to use nuclear weapons as an instrument of political coercion would increase. Were it to be perceived that both sides had first strike capability, the incentives to use nuclear weaons first in a crisis could be overwhelming.

At present few, if any, of the missiles of the two superpowers have the 'hard target capability' necessary for an effective disarming first strike. With the planned development of MX, Trident D5 and Pershing II missiles, however, the US is likely to remedy this 'gap' in the next few years. There is every likelihood that the Soviet Union will follow the American lead.

Trident D5 is the largest single programme in the US plans for acquiring a large-scale counter-silo, and therefore potentially first strike, capability. Using inertial guidance, stellar guidance, and inflight updating with Navstar satellites, the warheads are likely to attain a CEP* of 300 feet. This will give each Trident D5 warhead at least a 95% probability of destroying a hardened Soviet silo. Using two Trident warheads per Soviet silo, it has been estimated that only a handful of the 1378 Soviet land-based missiles would survive the initial attack.

In addition, it is possible that in the early 1990s, Trident D5 missiles will be fitted with a terminal guidance capability, enabling its warhead to home in even more precisely onto their targets. Such a capability is already being fitted to the Pershing II missiles now being deployed in West Germany. If used on Trident, it could reduce its CEP* to as low as 150 feet.

---

* CEP Circular Error Probable. The radius of a circle around a target within which 50% of warheads aimed at that target are predicated to land.

Missiles) of which only 670 are MIRVed.[14] Under the US *START* proposals, the two superpowers would cut their number of ballistic missiles to 850 each, of which no more than half (425) would be ICBMs. An additional sublimit of only 210 was proposed for the Soviet MIRVed ICBMs – the SS17, SS18 and SS19.[15]

If Trident is as accurate as its manufacturers claim, therefore, a British first strike could hope to destroy a very substantial proportion of existing Soviet ICBMs, including most of its most powerful ones (the MIRVed ICBMs). In the unlikely event of the Soviets agreeing to President Reagan's *START* proposals, Britain would be able to target independently *two* Trident warheads on most, if not all, ICBM silos: virtually ensuring their destruction.

It is likely that, even if *START* was accepted, Britain could not destroy each and every Soviet ICBM silo. In any event, there would still be other substantial nuclear forces available to retaliate against the UK, including medium range SS20 missiles, submarines, and bombers. But it is difficult to see how 896 Trident warheads can credibly be described as 'sufficient to target only a very small proportion of' 1378 ICBM silos.

'Decapitation'

Accurate missiles such as Trident D5 can not only be used to destroy ICBM silos. They can also – and perhaps more dangerously – be used against hardened Soviet command centres. So crucial are the latter that American analyst Paul Bracken recently argued:

> If only one shot at the king is allowed, point the pistol at his brain, not at his body...the best strategy may be to so paralyze and disrupt the enemy's command structure that his retaliation will be ragged and ineffective.
>
> Since the prospects for disarmament do not look good, perhaps the best mankind can hope for is to learn to live with the pervasive presence of nuclear weapons.
>
> Of all (the) alternatives, the decapitation strategy unfortunately may offer the best hope of escaping annihilation. The Soviet and American arsenals are so large and dispersed that a coordinated attack cannot hope to destroy enough of them to limit the retaliatory strike. But if such attacks were executed in conjunction with strikes against the command system many additional weapons might be paralysed into not retaliating. They could then be destroyed in later follow-on attacks, or they might remain dormant permanently. (This) might offer some small chance that no retaliation would follow.[16]

The potential for 'decapitation' that Trident would provide for Britain will be extremely dangerous and destabilising. For it may suggest a nuclear warfighting 'scenario' in which Britain could use its strategic force.

The number of weapons needed for a 'decapitation' attack is considerably smaller than those needed for a general disarming first strike. According to Paul Bracken, about one hundred highly accurate weapons would allow four or five warheads to be exploded on major command posts and would further destroy telephone switching centres, satellite ground stations, radars, and early warning stations. In addition, as few as 'ten high altitude high-yield nuclear bursts might be launched in conjunction with attacks on the national capital in order to generate strong EMP waves that could knock out communication and electrical power systems.' Finally, for extra assurance: 'Ground bursting of weapons would throw up radioactive dust, which could foul up airplane engines and disrupt reconstitution of the bombers.'

Were Britain to launch such an attack, even without a parallel US strike, it could cause such disruption that any large-scale Soviet response might be delayed. It would be likely that such a response *would* be forthcoming within hours, or at the most days, once the remnants of the Soviet military had realised what had happened. In such a situation it would therefore be 'rational' for the US to finish the job and destroy as many of the remaining Soviet nuclear weapons as quickly as possible in order to minimise the damage to the US itself.

The rationale of such a 'trigger' role for Britain's force will be discussed further in Chapter Four. It can be concluded here that a 'decapitation' strike against the Soviet Union will be well within the numerical capabilities of Britain's Trident force. Indeed, even if only two Trident boats are available, Britain will be able to launch over 400 highly accurate warheads at Soviet targets. These will be more than sufficient to destroy the 100 or so most crucial command and communications centres, generate further massive disruption through EMP and fallout effects, and leave tens or even hundreds of warheads for attacks on Soviet missile silos, submarine bases, and so on.

Launch on Warning?

There is considerable evidence that Soviet leaders are extremely worried by the possibility of a Western 'decapitation' strike. In the

Geneva negotiations on Intermediate Nuclear Forces (INF), now suspended, they made clear that they were more concerned by the 108 Pershing II missiles being deployed in Western Europe than by the 464 ground-launched cruise missiles (GLCMs). For the highly accurate Pershing II missiles could destroy the Soviet High Command's bunkers in the Moscow area within twelve minutes of launching from West Germany. There are suggestions that more Pershing IIs are to be deployed in West Germany in the mid 1980s, over and above the 108 so far announced, and there is a possibility that Pershing IIs will also be deployed in Alaska, within range of crucial Soviet Far Eastern military bases.[17]

Pershing II is, however, only a taster for what is to come. From the late 1980s onwards, Trident D5 will begin to be deployed in massive numbers by the US. By 1994, it is planned, the US will have 6,000 D5 warheads. By the end of the 1990s, Britain's deployment of up to 900 warheads should be complete. These warheads, if launched on depressed trajectory from waters near the USSR, will be able to destroy hardened targets in the Soviet Union within 10 minutes. Trident D5's flight-time can thus be much shorter than that of most other first strike weapons – such as MX (30 minutes) or cruise missiles (two to three hours). Also, unlike existing submarine-launched missiles – Polaris, Poseidon, Trident C4 – which cannot reliably destroy hardened targets, its guidance systems will make it an extremely effective counter-silo weapon. These two characteristics – short flight time and high accuracy – have led one US Congressman to describe Trident D5 as the most destabilizing (to superpower relations) 'first strike' weapon ever built, far more than the MX.[18]

In response to these new weapons, there is a danger – even a likelihood – that Soviet leaders will adopt one of several possible courses of action. They may place a proportion of their nuclear forces on a *Launch on Warning* posture, in which they would be fired on a (computer) warning that a large-scale attack was taking place. This would be designed to ensure that a disarming first strike by the US could not prevent the destruction of its own homeland. It would, however, have the disadvantage that it would increase the possibility of a nuclear war by accident, particularly during a crisis when both sides have their forces on alert. The unreliability of US strategic warning computers was illustrated in 1980 when a faulty computer chip led to an alert of US B52 nuclear bombers and the scrambling of airborne command posts.

If Launch-on-Warning is ruled out, Soviet leaders are likely to be forced to make preparations for *predelegation* and decentralisation of the authority to use nuclear weapons. Relatively low level commanders will have to assume that, in certain circumstances, they will be required to decide on their own that the nuclear weapons they control should be launched. (This procedure already appears to be in operation with Britain's Polaris missile submarines). In order for such decentralisation to be effective, some of the existing physical constraints on the unauthorised use of Soviet nuclear weapons may need to be removed. This – like Launch-on-Warning – is bound to increase the possibility of nuclear war by accident or miscalculation.

Finally, Soviet leaders may decide that, in the event of a crisis, their nuclear forces should be switched from a 'failsafe' to a '*faildeadly*' posture. 'Faildeadly' instructions have been considered in the past in wargames played by US senior officials.[19] It is not unlikely that their Soviet counterparts may have thought along similar lines. This will mean that, instead of launching only when receiving a authenticated coded message to do so, missile commanders will be instructed to launch unless they receive a periodic message *not* to do so. This will ensure that, if the national command centre is destroyed, some of the nuclear forces that do remain will be fired without a direct order.

These possible responses to the deployment of first strike weapons will mean that beyond a certain stage in a future crisis, the leaders of the nuclear powers may lose full control of the military machine. As in 1914, they may find themselves unable to stop the mobilisation of their forces for war. Realising that this is the case, they will face enormous pressures to minimise the damage to their own country by pushing the button first. The Trident programme – in the US and in the UK – will considerably increase the possibility of such a situation occurring.

Is Trident really 'independent'?

All the most important justifications for Britain possessing its own strategic nuclear force rest on the assumption that it is, in some sense, 'independent'. Yet, at the very least, there are important reasons for casting doubt on this assertion.

In the medium term Britain is heavily dependent on the United States for the retention of its nuclear force. Almost 50% of the expenditure on Trident will be on components bought in the US – the complete missile and re-entry systems, much of the submarine design work, and even 'certain warhead-related components'.[20]

When in service, Trident will depend on the US for continuing the supply of vital materials and components. These include

- *highly enriched uranium* for the submarines' nuclear reactors, which is supplied by the US under a 1958 agreement in return for UK supplies of plutonium for use in its own nuclear weapons.[21]
- *missile components and servicing*. Britain relies on the US to supply major components, such as rocket motors and solid propellants, for its missiles. Trident (unlike Polaris) will also rely on US facilities, at Kings Bay, Georgia, for the initial preparation for service of the missiles, and for their refurbishment at each major submarine refit every 7-8 years.[22]
- *periodic testing* of Trident's warheads at the Nevada underground site in order to ensure that they remain in sound condition.

Indeed, Trident actually *reduces* Britain's independence in several important respects. The continued US support for its nuclear force is dependent on Britain remaining a loyal partner. In particular there is a clear link between the acceptance of American nuclear bases on British soil and the American support of the UK 'independent deterrent.' In 1960, when Britain finally abandoned the attempt to manufacture a complete nuclear delivery system, the provision of the American *Skybolt* air-launched ballistic missile was linked to British agreement that the US could use the Holy Loch in Scotland for its own *Polaris* and *Poseidon* submarines.[23] It is doubtful whether if the UK had refused to accept the stationing of cruise missiles at Greenham Common and Molesworth it would have found an agreement on Trident obtainable. It would then have proved extremely costly for Britain to develop independently its own missile technology – even more expensive than Trident is likely to be. This added expense could well put Britain out of the nuclear race altogether: a consideration which helps to explain the lack of support for a British 'Gaullist' option. Such an option – retaining an independent nuclear force but removing American bases – has proven to be popular in France. There is little doubt that it would be also more politically acceptable in Britain – where public opposition to *British* nuclear weapons is much less than that to *American* nuclear bases. Were Britain to adopt such an option, however, not only would the costs be enormous. The degree of dependence is such that there would probably be a period of several years, after Polaris had gone out of service, in which Britain would have no effective strategic weapons system. Paradoxically, therefore, Britain can only remain an 'independent' nuclear power by allowing the stationing of nuclear weapons on its territory over which it has no control whatsoever.

Operational Independence

It is almost certainly the case that Britain's submarine-launched missiles are, and will be, independent in one rather limited sense. Mrs Thatcher, or her successor, after agreement with her Chiefs of Staff, can at any time give an order for these missiles to be fired, and the commanders of the submarines will, in all probability, obey those orders. That Britain's nuclear weapons could be used 'cold' in normal peacetime conditions is, however, so implausible as to be of marginal interest. The important question is whether Britain's independence of action can be retained in circumstances of intense crisis or war. Here the answer is much less clearcut.

Britain's dependence on the US does not stop at the supply of technology and equipment, or at the maintenance of key components of its weapons. There also appears to be a considerable degree of *operational* dependence. Details in this area are impossible to obtain. They constitute the most closely guarded secrets of the British state. It is therefore wise to be sceptical of those – even those in high office – who claim definitive knowledge of the question. Nevertheless it is clear that in three crucial areas – targeting, communications, and guidance – Britain is involved in substantial operational links with the United States.

Britain's nuclear forces form part of the nuclear forces available to NATO's SACEUR (Supreme Allied Commander, Europe), who is a US General. As such, they are assigned targets by a Joint Strategic Target Planning Staff (JSTPS) based at Omaha, Nebraska. Though precise details are unknown, British forces appear to form an integral part of the US plan for all-out nuclear war – its Single Integrated Operational Plan (SIOP). As part of SIOP, they would be used as part of a NATO nuclear war, limited or otherwise. In the late 1980s these operational plans will increasingly reflect the first strike capabilities of the US's new nuclear forces – MX, Trident D5, Pershing II, etc. Even if Britain's 'independent' nuclear targeting remains a predominantly countercity affair, it is probable that its Trident missiles will be assigned counterforce targets in *joint US-UK* plans.

It must be assumed that, in addition to joint targeting with the US, the British government does possess its own independent, non-NATO, targeting plans. In the absence of further information, however, it is difficult to assess how independent such plans are. Nuclear targeting requires a considerable degree of up-to-date intelligence on the position of potentially mobile enemy targets and of the state of enemy ballistic missile defences. Such information would be particularly crucial if British nuclear weapons were to be used in a relatively 'sophisticated' way against military targers rather than against immobile and indefensible cities. The UK at present appears to be heavily dependent on the US for the provision of such information. Britain cannot, and will not, be able to sustain the massive network of satellites, spy planes, and operatives which the US military controls. A withdrawal of US intelligence, therefore, would probably reduce the effectiveness of Britain's targeting procedures within a short period of time. If, as is possible if not likely, the British intelligence services are themselves highly penetrated by the US, then the possibility of British leaders obtaining the up-to-date and accurate information without US knowledge of their preparations would be further reduced.

These restrictions on targeting may not, in themselves, be crucial. While some information dates relatively quickly – eg on Soviet radar frequencies – much will be of use for months or even years. Since the value of Britain's force is officially held to be in destroying cities and other 'soft' targets – the location of which is well known – this may not be of great importance. The reliance on the US for intelligence may, however, reduce somewhat the feasibility of using Trident in a 'decapitation' attack. In a crisis the UK would find it difficult to know whether the Soviet leaders had relocated important command centres and other possible targets. Again, however, since the UK's aim in a 'decapitation attack' would be to 'trigger' a full US first strike, it is arguable whether such information would be necessary.

Britain's communications with its submarines are a second area in which its operational independence in a crisis must be questionable. Polaris (and, in future, Trident) is clearly 'British' in the sense that the decision to launch their missiles would be taken by the Prime Minister, along with at least one of his or her Chiefs of Staff. But the system for communicating these orders to submarines on parol are very vulnerable indeed. The main method of communications is Very Low Frequency (VLF) radio transmission, which can be picked up at least 10-15 metres underneath the sea. Britain possesses only three stations capable of transmitting such messages – at Rugby, Criggion and Anthorn (see map on p. 44). Yet these stations, together with any submarines in port at Faslane, could be easily, and quickly, 'taken out' by a Soviet, or indeed an American, surprise attack.

Even the future British *Skynet* satellites could be vulnerable to anti-satellite warfare. In the meantime it is pertinent to note that Britain relied heavily on United State military satellites to communicate with its forces during the 1982 Falklands War. Indeed the order to the submarine *HMS Conqueror* to sink the Argentine destroyer *General Belgrano* was itself probably communicated via an American satellite.[24]

It therefore seems that, in wartime, Britain could rapidly lose any independent links to its strategic submarines. Of course it is possible that other – unknown – methods of communication exist. These, however, might be vulnerable to pre-emptive and 'decapitation' attacks on Britain.

Finally, there is the question of submarine *navigation* and missile *guidance*. For a ballistic missile to be set on a correct trajectory towards its target(s), it must know where it is at any point in time, both before launch and, preferably, in midcourse. Trident will depend for such information on at least three separate systems. The first is the navigation system of the submarine itself, which 'keeps the fire control continuously up-dated with submarine position, course and speed in relation to potential targets.'[25]

Secondly, each Trident missile is likely to have a self-contained computer-operated stellar inertial guidance system. This will be programmed prior to launch with target information. Its purpose is to direct the missile during its flight to the point in space where the various re-entry vehicles are released.

Thirdly, the navigation and guidance systems of both the submarine and the missile will be complemented by the use of navigation satellites. The US is now deploying a new system called the Navstar Global Positioning System, comprising 18 satellites (plus 10 spares) in six 12-hour orbits. These will act as beacons enabling users to determine their positions to within 15 metres given the appropriate military code. Without this code, civilian users will only be able to position themselves to within 100 metres.[26]

All these three systems are American-supplied. They therefore impose a further degree of *medium-term* technical dependence on the UK. However, only one – Navstar – would not be within UK *operational* control. It is unclear whether recent proposals for a highly accurate European civilian positioning satellite (Navsat) will make dependence in this area less than absolute.

There must therefore be a large measure of doubt regarding the true meaning of Trident's 'independence'. In the last analysis, however, the question of operational independence hinges more on plausibility than on unknown technical factors. *Are there any circumstances in which Britain could use its nuclear weapons, or targets which it could profitably attack, when the US has chosen not to use its own nuclear forces? For if such circumstances or targets do not exist, and the British government were to believe that they could not, then Britain's nuclear force cannot be seen as an 'independent' one.* It is then reduced simply to a highly expensive and superfluous adjunct to the massive US arsenal. To answer these questions the next Chapter will explore some of the 'scenarios' in which, it has been argued, independent use is in fact possible, although there is widespread scepticism as the validity of any of them.

Even if such scenarios do exist, it is virtually certain that if the US does not wish to use its own nuclear weapons in a future crisis or against a particular target, then it will be strongly opposed to the UK doing so instead, particularly when British Trident missiles will be indistinguishable from American ones, and will be treated as such by the Soviet Union.

If such circumstances arise, therefore, the stakes will be such that the US will have an overwhelming interest in preventing a British use of nuclear weapons. This interest could be reflected not simply by denying intelligence and satellite channels, but also in sabotage of, and perhaps destruction of, British communications links and the submarines themselves. Indeed the faintest possibility of a British nuclear strike against the Soviets without US permission is likely to make British installations and submarines prime targets for nuclear strikes by *both* superpowers.

It is the vulnerability to such a US attack that, as much as any other factor, must cast doubt on Britain's claims to operational independence. It is a vulnerability that is, of course, never mentioned in public discussion because of its obvious diplomatic sensitivity, and the real extent of the 'problem' must be to a large extent a matter of speculation. Yet the deep involvement of the US in British military intelligence and communications – for example at GCHQ Cheltenham – suggests that the US will receive early warning of British preparations, and that it will have some capability for intercepting or blocking British communications with its nuclear forces.

It has been estimated that the US Navy usually knows the location of the Soviet Union's missile submarines to within 50 or 60 miles of their precise location by use of their sophisticated SOSUS (Sound Surveillance System).[27] Since the US co-operates with the UK on targeting – and thus on deployment – for its submarines, it is likely to know the location of the two or three British submarines at sea as well, if not better, than this. It would therefore be relatively straightforward technically to 'take out' Britain's strategic force if ballistic missiles were distributed over the entire segment of ocean in which the submarines were thought to be. Indeed Harold Brown, former US Secretary of Defense, has argued that 400 Soviet one-megaton warheads could boil the sea within a diameter of 100 miles, destroying any submarine within the area.[28]

The inability of Britain's nuclear force to be able to continue operations in the face of US opposition – and even attack – casts serious doubt on its operational independence. As we shall see in Chapter Five, there are also ground for arguing that it is impossible to envisage a situation in which such operational independence would in fact be useful. A combination of realities which leaves most of us asking 'what is Trident for?'

Chapter Four
Trident: What Is It For?

For the US, the main purpose of the Trident D5 programme is relatively clear. It is to improve its capability for attacking 'hard' targets in the Soviet Union in a nuclear war. If both Trident and MX are deployed, by the early 1990s the US will be able to destroy virtually all Soviet ICBM silos simultaneously in a pre-emptive strike. This capability to fight and 'win' a nuclear war, it is argued, will in turn give the US greater political leverage in the global contest with the Soviet Union. As influential strategist Colin Gray has argued:

> If American nuclear power is to support US foreign policy object-
> ives, the US must possess the ability to wage nuclear war rationally
> ... The US should plan to defeat the Soviet Union and to do so at a
> cost that would not prohibit recovery... Once the defeat of the
> Soviet state is established as a war aim, defense professionals should
> attempt to identify an optimum targeting plan for the accomplish-
> ment of that goal... and intelligent US offensive strategy, wedded
> to homeland defenses, should reduce US casualties to approxim-
> ately 20 million, which should render US strategic threats more
> credible.[1]

Targeting Trident

Is the role of Britain's Trident force to be compared with that of the US force? Not according to government statements. Ministers have repeatedly insisted that Britain has no such sophisticated intentions, and that 'the reasons behind the UK and US decisions to deploy D5 are very different.'[2] While the US force, it is admit-ted, is designed to destroy missile silos and other hard targets, Britain's force is described simply as a 'last resort deterrent' like Polaris.

Yet such an argument is hopelessly flawed. Britain's Trident forces will, like Polaris at present, be committed to NATO and tar-geted in accordance with US strategic policy 'save where Britain's supreme national interests otherwise require.' Trident will be fully integrated into US plans for nuclear warfighting with target-ing plans based on the capabilities – such as improved accuracy – which Trident will possess. For the British government to imply otherwise is to suggest that Trident would, on the day, never be used in accordance with NATO plans. If that were so, it implies that the 'contribution to NATO' concept, and the joint targeting staff in Omaha, are really a facade only necessary to reassure the Americans that the British force is not so independent after all.

Not only is Britain's Trident force likely to be given first strike roles as part of US strategic plans. It also seems likely that Britain's independent, or non-NATO, targeting will follow American trends towards nuclear warfighting doctrines. There is a strong, and repeated, tendency for military planners to seek to use weapon systems to the maximum of their capabilities. As the evolution of US policy has demonstrated, nuclear strategy and targeting policy have been decisively influenced by the technological possibilities available. There is little reason to suppose that such forces will not also affect British decision makers.

So far as is known, there has been no formal decision to change Britain's independent targeting policy. However, unlike the relatively open discussion in the US, Britain has been extremely secretive in this area. The 1980 Open Government Document stated simply that:

> Successive UK Governments have always declined to make public their nuclear targeting policy and plans, or to define precisely what minimum level of destructive capability they judged necessary for deterrence. The Government however thinks it right now to make clear that their concept of deterrence is concerned essentially with *posing a potential threat to key aspects of Soviet state power*. There might with changing conditions be more than one way of doing this and some flexibility in contingency planning is appropriate.[3] (Author's emphasis)

It is clear from semi-official sources that the ability to destroy Moscow is considered to be a necessary, though not a sufficient, part of these plans. What is unspecified is whether 'key aspects of state power' might, at some future date, also include military targets such as missile silos. This possibility was discussed in 1980, by Michael Quinlan, the senior civil servant in charge of Britain's strategic nuclear programmes, in evidence to the Commons Defence Committee:

Patrick Wall (Conservative MP)
Is Trident going to be sufficiently accurate to switch from the softer to the harder targets? I am asking about Trident I. I will come on to Trident II afterwards.

Mr Quinlan
I hesitate to get deeply into the question of targeting...Polaris, in
its various forms, will not have the kind of accuracy that will make
it any good at taking on silos at any reasonable rate of exchange, but
there is a range of targets between hitting a large city and hitting a
silo which may be of some relevance. The Trident memorandum
...does use a general term – Soviet state power – which may
embrace a range of targets lying between these two.[4]

Unfortunately, Mr Quinlan was not pressed further on Trident II
targeting. Nevertheless it is clear that even the present force is
already targeted on a range of military and non-military targets, in
order to provide British leaders with a number of so-called 'limited
nuclear options'. Once Trident II gives Britain a better 'rate of
exchange' against missile silos and command bunkers, there is
little reason to suppose that these too will not be included in the
government's options.

Nuclear strategists have argued for some years that greater
'flexibility' in the targeting of British (and French) nuclear forces
would increase their deterrent value. Graeme Auton has argued
this point in some detail:

Medium powers must escape the kind of logic asserting that the
only effective targets for smaller deterrents are cities and civilian
populations; ie, they must reject the contradictory notion that
medium nuclear powers have a deterrent value but no war-fighting
utility. Required is a range of options allowing for the measured
and selective employment of nuclear weapons against a wide array
or targets, in order to avoid immediate escalation to a level of
destruction that could not credibly be pursued.

In the event of a Warsaw Pact conventional assault on Western
Europe, or some other limited provocation, the British and French
governments would have an initial option...of striking at vulnerable counterforce targets in the Soviet Union.

These targets would include:

Non-military, industrial targets outside urban centres that would
require only one or two nuclear warheads each. Air-defence
sites..., military airfields, major army bases and submarine bases
[in which perhaps half of all Soviet SSBNs would be docked or
undergoing refit]. Hard targets such as missile silos, nuclear
weapons storage facilities and command posts.

Reassuringly, Mr Auton tells us that:

Of course the USSR might launch limited counterforce or otherwise 'selective' retaliatory strikes of its own...to demoralize
European populations without inviting condign destruction of
Soviet cities. The assumption is, however, that at this point there
would be powerful incentives on both sides for controlling conflict
and preventing its escalation to mutual city targeting.

Since the initial use of nuclear weapons (by the UK) would not
have apocalyptic consequences, the threat to resort to it in the event
of dire provocation would be more credible – much more credible,
certainly, than the threat of massive countercity strikes.[5]

Such arguments are dangerous madness. They assume that a
nuclear war can be kept limited even when dozens, perhaps hundreds, of nuclear weapons are landing on Soviet territory.[6] They
assume that leaders who had demonstrated themselves to be foolhardy enough to start a nuclear war would then have the sense to
cease fighting after millions had been killed (as even a 'limited' war
would imply). Yet it is on such assumptions that current NATO
defence policy is based.

Indeed support for Trident undoubtedly comes partly from its
ability to make limited nuclear options technically more feasible.
Trident's increased range, the greated number of submarines
available, and the MIRVing of its warheads all make it more feasible to use only a proportion of the nuclear arsenal in a 'warning'
attack on selected targets – withholding the remaining weapons in
order to threaten escalation to counter-city strikes. The increased
accuracy of the missiles, in addition, provides an ability to attack
hardened targets in the initial 'controlled' exchange.

An influential study of the targeting requirements for Britain's
nuclear forces, written by Geoffrey Kemp and published by the
International Institute for Strategic Studies, gives some insight
into this trend in thinking. It starts with a lengthy discussion on
the most cost-effective way for Britain to destroy major Soviet
cities which includes the chilling argument that:

It can be argued that *more* chaos would result from a nuclear attack
that only partially destroyed a city and left many injured to be cared
for than from an attack that totally obliterated it, leaving few, if any,
survivors.

Kemp concludes his study by contending that:

Any decision by medium powers to develop forces capable of fairly
sophisticated targeting options...(would be expensive)...How-
ever it can be argued that such an option would give a medium-

power nuclear force greater political flexibility in event of a major conflict with the Soviet Union or (perhaps more important) in a pre-war crisis situation.[7]

More recently David Hobbs at Aberdeen University, in a study designed to investigate less expensive alternatives to Trident, discusses the minimum requirements for such an alternative:

> ...the United Kingdom might be well advised to seek a more flexible retaliatory capability, allowing some scope for controlled or graduated escalation (for intra-war deterrence). That would imply a wider range of target options, taking advantage of the enhanced accuracy of new delivery vehicles; and, if practicable, a less discrete system than the existing one, so that use of a portion of it would not automatically jeopardise the remainder.

As a result of this logic, Mr Hobbs then argues that an alternative to Trident must be able to destroy both the 'area' targets for which Polaris is intended and, in addition, a number of counterforce targets. He concludes by defining the 'criterion for adequacy' for such an alternative as '100 assuredly arriving warheads' – more than three times the targeting capability of the current Polaris force, even with two boats on patrol.

Finally, advocates of a British move towards counterforce are now making an attempt to add a moral gloss to their case by invoking, and grossly misinterpreting, the Christian doctrine of the 'just war'. This was evident recently in the forthright views of Julian Critchley, MP, Vice Chairman of the Conservative Party's Defence Committee, who quotes the Second Ecumenical Council of the Vatican in support of his contention that:

> Morally there is all the difference in the world, and one far deeper than the terms 'counterforce' or 'countervalue' imply, between indiscriminate massacre of men, women and children and the aiming of a weapon at a particular military objective, whatever collateral damage it may cause.
>
> If, as I think probable, both the technical expertise of accurate nuclear targeting and the growth of moral repugnance to the policy of wholesale slaughter combine to exclude the latter from the planned deterrence of the Atlantic Alliance, nothing but good could come from making it clear to the public. For it is the vision of Hiroshima on the grand scale that feeds the hysterical fear which weakens the national will. Yet the nuclear holocaust, beloved of the CND propagandist, is in reality a most improbable event.[9]

Or, in more simple language, we should learn to love the Bomb!

Were Trident to go ahead, we can expect British policy to move in the direction indicated by these writers. It would be improbable for the British military to deliberately abstain from making plans for counterforce targeting options, when it has the capacity to do so. Since these options are a central part of SIOP – to which Trident will normally be committed – the probability must be further diminished. The deployment of Trident will therefore, almost certainly, mean a substantial shift in British nuclear planning towards a nuclear warfighting and counterforce policy.

The move from a countercity policy to one of 'limited nuclear options' and counterforce, however, will not substantially resolve the more fundamental questions. What is Trident for? In what circumstances would it be used? For, in order for Trident to have any military – or 'deterrent' – value, there must not only be a *technical* possibility that it can be used independently – and the discussion in Chapter 3 threw some doubt on that. There must also be some '*scenarios*' in which Britain would be prepared to use its strategic nuclear force when the US did not wish to use its own. If such a scenario did not exist, there would be no conceivable justification for the expenditure of over £10,000 million on a force whose only role would then be as a marginal increment to the massive overkill that already exists in the US SIOP arsenal.

Advocates of Trident are convinced that such 'scenarios' do exist. The government paper which announced the decision to purchase Trident I argues that:

> We need to convince the Soviet leaders that even if they thought that at some critical point as a conflict developed the US would hold back, the British force could still inflict a blow so destructive that the penalty for aggression would have proved too high.
>
> A force which could strike tellingly only if the US also did so – which plainly relied, for example, on US assent to its use, or an attenuation or distraction of Soviet defences by US forces – would not achieve the purpose.[10]

Various scenarios in which Britain's Trident force might be used on its own have been suggested. There is the 'second centre' argument, which is particularly popular in official justifications of the Trident decision. Then there is the 'sanctuary' argument, which is perhaps the most popular amongst those unconstrained by considerations of diplomacy. Thirdly, there is the 'last resort' scenario in which British nuclear weapons would be used to deter either invasion, or nuclear devastation, of the British Isles themselves. And, finally, there is the 'trigger' argument, which is used to add to the credibility of the force in each of these three main scenarios. Since it is the possibility of credible use of Trident that forms the basis of the intellectual argument for its purchase, it is necessary to examine critically each of these rationales in turn.

NATO's Second Centre

The 'second centre' argument is based on the proposition that the Soviet Union is likely to be more deterred from aggression against Western Europe if there are two centres of nuclear decision-making within NATO than if there were only one. It is an argument that is the most popular in official justifications as it enables the government to present its independent nuclear force as a contribution to Western defence, rather than as a diversion from it. It is argued that:

> A Soviet leadership... might believe that it could impose its will on Europe by military force without becoming involved in strategic nuclear war with the US. Modernised US nuclear forces in Europe help guard against any such misconception; but an independent capability fully under European control provides a key element of insurance. A nuclear decision would of course be no less agonising for the UK than for the US. But it would be the decision of a separate and independent power, and a power whose survival in freedom would be directly and immediately threatened by aggression in Europe.[11]

The diplomatic attraction of such an argument is clear. Yet it is difficult to believe that it holds much water even in government circles. For it requires the assumption that the UK might be willing – in some circumstances – to use its own nuclear weapons, when the US had refused to use its own, *in defence of other European countries*. In these, undefined, circumstances Britain's nuclear 'umbrella' over West Germany would deter the Soviet Union while that of the US did not.

In justification of the 'second centre' role, it is argued that, should NATO's forces – including most of the UK's Army and Air Force – be losing in conventional war in Central Europe, Britain should – or at least could – use its own nuclear weapons to avert defeat. It might start with a 'demonstration shot' to indicate British willingness to raise the conflict to a nuclear level. If this proved unsuccessful, the UK would then escalate to use of theatre nuclear weapons (such as Tornado) or to a limited counterforce attack on Soviet targets (with Trident). Finally, if all else failed, a

selective attack on Soviet cities might persuade the Kremlin
leaders to see the error of their ways and withdraw.

Such a ladder of nuclear escalation, it is argued, is credible
because Britain has a more direct national interest in Europe than
the US, whose territorial security would not be so immediately
threatened. This interest, in turn, means that Britain could be
more willing to risk nuclear destruction in defence of Europe than
the US. This possibility, it is argued, will deter the Soviet Union
from a conventional invasion more than the US nuclear 'deterrent'
by itself. Indeed, the government argues, Trident would add more
to deterrence of such an invasion than would a 50% increase in the
British Army's conventional forces in Germany:

> The presence of an independent deterrent under the absolute con-
> trol of the British Prime Minister greatly multiplies the risk to any
> potential aggressor of starting a war in Europe. Those who argue
> that the expenditure on Trident would be better devoted to streng-
> thening our conventional forces must consider whether a future
> Soviet leadership are more likely to be deterred by an invulnerable
> second strike submarine-launched ballistic missile force or, for
> example, by two extra armoured divisions with 300 additional
> tanks . . . [12]

The 'second centre' argument may appeal to officials and politicians
anxious to demonstrate Britain's loyalty to NATO. But is it really
credible to suppose that a British government would order the first
use of nuclear weapons, when the US had not done so, and in defence
of other European countries? Or that the Soviets would believe that
it would do so? Such a decision would have to be made in the knowledge that a previously unscathed Britain would then, in all likelihood, face swift and appalling casualties in a Soviet counter-attack. It
is thus impossible to believe that a Soviet leadership which was prepared to risk American nuclear first-use might be deterred from a
conventional invasion by the existence of a British force. A perceived
NATO ability to halt such an invasion by non-nuclear means would
be more likely to have the desired effect.

The Sanctuary

The 'sanctuary' argument is, in a sense, the opposite of the 'second
centre' one. While proponents of the latter argue that Britain's
nuclear force could protect its allies by threatening to *start* a
nuclear war in Europe, sanctuary supporters, by contrast, argue

that it could be used to *exclude* Britain from such a war. It is argued that, were nuclear war to start in Europe, the two superpowers would have a strong incentive to exclude their own territories from such a war. Certainly the US government appears to believe that it is possible to fight a nuclear war limited to Europe. An independent British force, it is argued, would give the UK's territory immunity from such a war much as the possession of nuclear weapons by the two superpowers gives their homelands some protection.

The 'sanctuary' argument is particularly favoured by those (including a powerful lobby in the Conservative Party) who seek a more nationalist approach to defence policy. They resent Britain's dependence on the US, and are envious of France, with its independent nuclear force clearly devoted to national, rather than NATO, 'defence'. They would, in principle at least, prefer a 'Fortress Britain' policy, in which Britain withdrew its troops from Germany, expelled US bases, and concentrated its resources on a truly independent nuclear force and on a strong Navy.[13] Even if these steps are not possible, they support the possession of Polaris/Trident in British control in the belief that it will give the government in Whitehall increased influence in a crisis and will deter the Soviet Union – and the US – from including the British Isles in the nuclear battlefield.

This is an unconvincing argument for a number of reasons. Most fundamentally, it rests on the untenable assumption that a nuclear war could be geographically limited to continental Europe. Yet the weight of considered evidence suggests that, once such a war had started, and hundreds, perhaps thousands, of nuclear weapons had been detonated, it would be impossible to control. Politicians would rapidly lose communications with, and thus control over, the thousands of theatre nuclear weapons in Europe. Enormous incentives would be created, on both sides, to launch a disarming first strike against the other's strategic nuclear forces in order to minimise damage in an all-out holocaust.

Even if it were conceivably possible that a nuclear war could be limited to Europe the presence of US 'theatre' nuclear forces would ensure that Britain was not excluded from the battlefield. The British Isles are packed with bases whose main role in war would be to enable the US to fight a limited nuclear war: the cruise missiles being deployed at Greenham Common, the F-111 bombers at Upper Heyford and Lakenheath, the Poseidon submarines at Holy Loch, and so on (see figure 4). It is incredible to suggest that the Soviet Union will not attack US bases in Britain were the US to attempt to fight a limited nuclear war in which

Figure 4:
Britain: a Nuclear Bullseye

Note: Only the most important targets
associated with the American nuclear forces
in the British Isles are shown.

these bases would play a key role. If it did launch selective nuclear strikes against these bases, it is difficult to see what advantage Britain would achieve from retaliation against the Soviet homeland. It would invite only a further, more devastating, attack.

Those who are concerned at the possibility of a limited nuclear war in Europe, and how to keep Britain out of it, would do better to advocate the removal from this country of the American and British nuclear bases designed for such a conflict. Such a measure could not guarantee the exclusion of the UK from a theatre nuclear war. It would, however, remove the priority targets in such a war; and thus reduce both the probability of, and the size of, any nuclear attack.

Britain standing alone

If Trident has no credible purpose in a European war between NATO and the Soviet Union – either as a 'second centre' or a 'sanctuary' – could it nevertheless have a role if Britain were to *stand alone* in a future crisis?

There are two categories of scenarios in which, it has been suggested, this could indeed be the case. Firstly, it is possible that, in a future crisis outside Europe, Britain's nuclear weapons could be used in order to coerce a non-nuclear state into accepting British demands. Such a use would not require national suicide. It might therefore, in some circumstances, be credible and indeed 'rational'. Secondly, it is argued, the politics of Europe and the US may not remain static into the indefinite future, and the government must also ensure against the possibility that the Soviet Union might dominate Europe either by direct military conquest or political 'subversion'. In such circumstances an independent nuclear force may, it is believed, deter the Soviets from attacking the British Isles themselves.

Using Trident in the Third World?

There is a temptation to dismiss the possibility of Britain's nuclear weapons being used in the Third World as so improbable as to be unworthy of discussion. A crisis outside Europe could not, on any reasonable definition, be seen as affecting Britain's vital national interests. Indeed there must be considerable doubt whether there should be any role for the British armed forces outside the NATO area, with the possible exception of UN peacekeeping operations.

Certainly a British use, or threat to use, nuclear weapons against a non-nuclear power would be quite disproportionate to any political or economic benefits that could be obtained. It would generate enormous pressures for rapid acquisition of nuclear forces by non-nuclear states. It would lead to a considerable increase in international tension. The government, in contemplating such actions, would have to take into account the possibility that it could escalate into a wider – and catastrophic – conflict.

Despite the implausibility and immorality of such a role, however, it is a role which the United States at least has considered on several occasions since 1945. Not, it must be added, with great success. Daniel Ellsberg has cited over a dozen crises in which the United States has threatened to use nuclear weapons.[14]

Nor is the US the only country which has contemplated the use of nuclear weapons in the Third World. There is also evidence that Britain's nuclear forces were seen as a cheap way of defending its Empire in the 1950s and 1960s. It was believed that the 'A' bomb provided a means of defending the far-flung Empire without expensive conscript forces. In 1957, Macmillan argued that: 'The end of conscription must depend on reliance on nuclear weapons.' To reinforce this point, British nuclear bombers were assigned to defend the Middle East from the Cyprus base, and hints of their possible use in the developing conflict with Indonesia were made. Minister of Defence Duncan Sandys announced that nuclear weapons would be available for the defence of South-East Asia, and that nuclear-capable Canberra bombers would be going to Malaya.[15]

Nor was the imperial function of Britain's nuclear force exhausted when Labour came into office in October 1964. Within weeks of entering office Harold Wilson, the new Prime Minister, offered a nuclear 'umbrella' to India. Part of the V-bomber force was specifically excluded from plans for NATO, and the 1965 Defence White Paper announced that:

> The Chinese nuclear explosion casts a new shadow over the future making it more difficult to forecast the trend of political development in an area where we have Commonwealth and treaty responsibilities to assist our friends ... *Our nuclear policy must help to provide some reassurance to non-nuclear powers* (Author's emphasis)

Unsurprisingly the Indian government rejected the offer.[16]

Most dramatically, there have been several reports which suggest that the use of nuclear weapons may have been seriously considered during the war with Argentina in April-May 1982. According to Tam Dalyell, MP, a heated debate had taken place in

Whitehall in early April, as the Task Force prepared to sail, on whether nuclear weapons should be carried on the fleet. Eventually, it appears, nuclear weapons were carried, although in reduced numbers, some of which later sank with HMS Sheffield.[17]

Moreover, possible plans may not have been confined to the use of tactical nuclear weapons – such as depth charges – against Argentine submarines. There have also been reports that during the conflict one of Britain's Polaris submarines was diverted to a position south of Ascension Island – within range of Argentine cities but out of range of the Soviet Union.[18]

These reports are in my view substantially correct. They have been given credence in off-the-record reports by senior political and military figures involved. Indeed sacked Navy Minister, Keith Speed, MP, stated on *NewsNight* that he would be most surprised if the fleet were not carrying nuclear weapons. The government's insistence that it 'could neither confirm nor deny the presence of nuclear weapons in any particular location' reinforces the credibility of these reports.[19]

Perhaps Professor Neville Brown of Birmingham University had these circumstances in mind in 1983 when he referred to 'the British sense that a tactical nuclear capability may have some background relevance to "out-of-area" operations.'[20]

1940 Revisited

While the use of Britain's nuclear weapons outside Europe must therefore remain a possibility, however, it cannot be used openly as a justification for Britain retaining its independent 'deterrent'. The public opposition to its use would be too great, as indeed Nixon realised when he pulled back from using nuclear weapons in Vietnam in 1969. For most people it is only in circumstances where the British Isles themselves are under direct threat that, perhaps, the independent strategic force would have a role. In such circumstances, where Britain stood alone as it did in 1940, it is argued that Polaris/Trident could indeed deter an enemy considering invasion or bombardment. As the Ministry of Defence argues:

> In the last resort, if the Alliance was to collapse, the possession of an independent strategic weapon provides the UK with the means of preserving national security by deterring large scale conventional or nuclear attack or of countering nuclear blackmail.[21]

Yet the threat to use nuclear weapons in such a 'scenario' would be neither desirable nor plausible. For it would be suicidal for the British government to carry out such a threat. As a result, a Soviet government would be unlikely to be deterred by it. For such a desperate situation to be reached in the first place, it must be assumed that the Red Army had successfully overrun Western Europe without the conflict escalating to nuclear war.

If the Soviet Union had already taken considerable risks – including that of nuclear conflict – in conquering Western Europe, an implausible British nuclear threat would carry little weight. It would be unnecessary for the Soviets to use its nuclear weapons in order to defeat Britain. It could launch a conventional invasion with a high probability of success – particularly if most of the British Army and Air Force had been destroyed in the continental campaign.

In these circumstances, would the British government be foolish enough to initiate a nuclear war with a superpower – even with tactical weapons against an invasion fleet? And, more importantly if we are concerned with 'deterrence', would a Soviet leadership reckless enough to invade Germany and France believe a British threat to do so? The answer must be no. British use of nuclear weapons would in these circumstances, be certain to bring swift nuclear retaliation. If such retaliation was limited – perhaps against nuclear submarine bases – Britain would be no better off than when it started in 'deterrence' terms, and with several hundred thousand casualties as a warning against further nuclear strikes. If, on the other hand, the Soviets responded with a comprehensive pre-emptive attack against Britain's command and communication centres and its military facilities then there would be nothing left to defend. The British people – and, in all probability, their foolhardy leaders – would be radioactive dust.

Surely it would be infinitely preferable for Britain, if threatened with invasion, to mount as determined a non-nuclear defence as possible rather than resort to suicidal nuclear threats. It would have at its disposal the natural geographical advantage that it is an island, thus making viable coastal defences extremely important. It could mobilise the population for an inch-by-inch defence of territory once an invader had managed to land. It could, by these means, impose a tremendous cost on an invader which, it would be hoped, could postpone an attack until other nations – notably the US – were able to come to Britain's aid with transatlantic conventional reinforcements.

A capability for imposing a high 'entry price' would not necessarily succeed in deterring invasion. If the Soviets did invade Britain, the casualties would be considerable with the end result, in all probability, a resounding defeat. But there would at least be a chance to fight back. The Soviet Union, which already suffers from a backward economy and disaffection in Eastern Europe, would find its armed forces overstretched and prone to defection if obliged to police an affluent, but hostile, Western population. No empire in history has lasted for ever. This one would probably be one of the more short lived.

A non-nuclear defence, therefore, would not only offer some chance of deterring invasion. It would also, if unsuccessful, give the British people another chance in the future to regain their freedom. It must, therefore, be infinitely preferable to so-called nuclear 'defence' which in reality is nothing more than a sophisticated and implausible doomsday machine.

Nuclear Blackmail

If it would be an act of madness to use Britain's nuclear force to deter invasion, could it nevertheless at least deter a nuclear attack on the British Isles? This is the justification offered by John Nott, when Secretary of State for Defence, to a House of Commons Committee:

> (Trident) could not conceivably be a first strike weapon. It is there as an ultimate defence of this country against a nuclear strike, a pre-emptive strike by a nuclear power.[22]

It is implausible, in the first place, why the Soviets would need to threaten the first use of nuclear weapons against Britain were it left to defend itself. The Soviets' overwhelming superiority in conventional forces would be sufficient to ensure it victory. Moreover, this 'scenario' assumes that Britain would be 'standing alone' against a continent dominated by the Soviet army. In such circumstances the Soviet Union would already, it must be assumed, have conquered NATO's armies in Western Europe without triggering a nuclear holocaust. Would it then be likely to risk the latter by threatening the use of its nuclear weapons against Britain? A conventional invasion would appear to be a much more logical, and less risky, step to take. As already discussed, British nuclear weapons can provide no deterrent to that.

Moreover, advocates of an 'independent deterrent' often fail to take into account the considerable constraints that exist on the threat to use nuclear weapons against non-nuclear powers. Despite the large number of conflicts since 1945, there have been few such cases of 'nuclear blackmail'. Those that have occurred – such as Nixon's threat against Vietnam – have failed when their bluff was called.[23] The reason such threats fail is that the first use of nuclear weapons since 1945 – and against a non-nuclear nation – would have incalculable *political* costs for the aggressor. It would lead to a massive shift in world opinion against it, and would cause tremendous revulsion amongst its own people. Any government contemplating such action would have to consider the likely reaction – massive rearmament by non-occupied countries, rebellions in satellite states, and mounting dissatisfaction at home.

It is perhaps plausible that a superpower would be willing to bear these costs if the gain to be achieved by nuclear blackmail were the defeat of the other superpower and/or effective world domination. If it were designed simply, however, to defeat a minor power – such as Britain – the balance of advantage is likely to be quite different. Calling a nuclear blackmailer's bluff might therefore actually work – as the Vietnamese found in 1969. At the same time, if the aggressor was believed to be ready to use nuclear weapons, there would be no alternative *whether or not Britain possessed its own.* It would be more rational to accede to the demands of the enemy, and continue the struggle once Britain is occupied, than to allow the total annihilation of the British people to take place.

Indeed in some respects immunity to nuclear blackmail is likely to be greater for a non-nuclear power. For the use of nuclear weapons against a nuclear power could be 'justified' – at least domestically – as a pre-emptive and 'defensive' action to protect the 'aggressor's' own population against retaliation. Indeed this argument is still employed by some US officials as a rationale for a disarming first strike on the Soviet Union. With Britain retaining hundreds of weapons on its soil – British and American – the Soviet Union can justify an attack with nuclear weapons more easily than against, say, non-nuclear Sweden.

There are strong political constraints on breaking the implicit moratorium on the use of nuclear weapons that has existed since 1945. While, thankfully, this moratorium exists, the foremost consideration must be how to strengthen these constraints further. In Britain's case at least, this can be done most effectively by renouncing its own nuclear weapons and adopting a non-suicidal and thus non-nuclear defence policy. By this example, it can make a modest, but perhaps vital, contribution to stopping the dangerous process of nuclear proliferation.

Britain's nuclear trigger

The weakness of the 'scenarios' in which Britain's nuclear weapons could be used should now be apparent. The idea that Britain would use its nuclear weapons first in response to a Soviet conventional attack on Germany (the 'second centre' argument) is not taken seriously even within the Government. The notion that Britain's nuclear weapons could allow it to be a 'sanctuary' is based on the unlikely assumption that the superpowers would be able to prevent a nuclear war, once started, from rapidly escalating to a global holocaust. With the massive US nuclear presence in Britain, it is an argument that loses all credibility. Finally, the argument that Britain's nuclear weapons could be used if it were 'standing alone' does not stand up to serious examination. It would be clearly unacceptable to use them in situations – such as the Falklands War – where vital national interests were not immediately at stake. Yet when such interests could be at stake – for example, if the Soviet Union were threatening to invade – the use of nuclear weapons would ensure certain national suicide.

In an attempt to add some strength to these extremely dubious 'scenarios' for its use, supporters of Trident have invoked its possible role as a 'trigger' for the much larger US nuclear force. It is argued that the use of Britain's Trident missiles against the Soviet Union could not be distinguished from an attack from the US Trident force. The Soviets would be likely to respond as if the attack did come from the US. In these circumstances, it would be 'rational' for the US to attack first, destroy as many Soviet nuclear missiles as possible, and thus to some extent limit the damage to itself.

This argument will be strengthened by Trident's 'decapitation' capability. For a British attack on Soviet command and control centres might delay retaliation for some time, perhaps several hours. Were Britain to launch such an attack, there would be overwhelming pressure for the US to pre-empt such a response and utterly destroy all remaining Soviet nuclear forces. Indeed such a possibility is implicit in the British government's own discussion of the Trident decision:

> ...one practical approach to judging how much deterrent power Britain needs is to consider what type and scale of damage Soviet leaders might think likely to leave them critically handicapped afterwards in continuing confrontation with a relatively unscathed United States.[24]

The trigger argument is, of course, never discussed openly by government Ministers or officials. It could hardly be otherwise. For it is a glaring paradox that the US should be helping Britain retain a force whose military purpose, if it can be said to have one, would be to involve the US in a nuclear holocaust against its will. Official discussion of the 'trigger' argument would highlight, in an uncomfortable way, whether or not Trident would really be 'independent', and in particular whether the US could pre-emptively destroy Britain's nuclear force if necessary. It is hardly a public discussion that the British government wishes to promote.

The Real Reasons for Trident

Trident's possible ability to trigger a global holocaust, rather than simply a European one, does not in any way add to its value. The use of nuclear weapons by Britain in any circumstances would still be a deeply irrational act. A 'triggered' US first strike could not hope to destroy all Soviet forces. Even if direct nuclear retaliation on the UK were limited, the ensuing 'nuclear winter' would condemn survivors to a prolonged holocaust. There can be no purpose in the use of nuclear weapons.

The realisation that Britain's nuclear force can have no military purpose is shared even by many of its supporters. The *real* reasons for the Trident decision lie in large part elsewhere. For, despite its lack of military value, the 'independent' nuclear force remains a powerful symbol for those obsessed with Britain's international status. In the last four decades, Britain's leaders have presided over the collapse of an Empire and a precipitate economic and industrial decline. They desperately yearn for some compensation, some assurance that Britain is still a Great Power. Trident appeals to these sentiments. Its value as a political symbol in peacetime comes, not so much in Britain's relations with the Soviet Union, as in its relations with its capitalist allies. It allows our leaders to believe they are still a notch above 'second-rate' non-nuclear powers such as Germany and Japan. It also reinforces the erroneous idea that we still have a 'special relationship' with the US, giving the British Prime Minister privileged access to the President during a crisis.

Most important of all, perhaps, Trident is seen by our military and political elite as essential in preserving Britain's position in Europe. The thought of England's historical rival, France, being the only independent nuclear power in Europe still gives apoplexies to admirals and generals reared on institutional memories of Trafalgar and Waterloo. Even Field-Marshal Lord Carver, one of the most prominent critics of Britain and NATO's reliance on nuclear weapons, argued in 1980 that:

> I see no military need for us to have our own nuclear weapons...
> Why do I not therefore follow the logic...and advocate what Lord
> Hill-Norton describes as 'unilateral nuclear disarmament'? For the
> very reasons that have influenced successive British governments
> whatever their political colour. Because of the profound *political*
> impact it would have in the country, among our allies, on our
> potential enemies and in the world at large. *Certainly as long as
> France retains a similar capability*, it would symbolize a renuncia-
> tion of power and influence, a desire to step out of the front line, to
> shoulder less responsibility for the burden of dealing with the
> world's problems.[25]

Proponents of nuclear disarmament, in contrast, would argue that it is in its 'profound political impact' that the renunciation of Britain's nuclear force would yield the greatest benefits.

The illusion of Britain's continuing 'Great Power' status, which has underpinned the commitment to nuclear weapons since the 1940s, is a powerful one. Yet it is also one that has prevented Britain's leaders from adjusting to its real position in the world, with further economic decline as the result. Only when such misplaced notions of Britain's international status are abandoned can we look forward to a reversal of that decline. The renunciation of Britain's own strategic nuclear weapons would be a major contribution to this much needed shift in attitudes.

Chapter Five

The Costs

Trident will not only be a useless status symbol. It will also be a very expensive one. Official estimates of its cost have risen steadily in the last four years. In 1980, the cost of the Trident I programme was estimated at between £4,500 million and £5,000 million at July 1980 prices. In 1982, when the decision to switch to D5 was announced, the cost rose to £7,500 million at September 1981 prices. The latest estimate, made in March 1984, revised this again to £8,729 million at September 1983 prices:[1] more than £160 for every man, woman and child in the United Kingdom.

Yet this official estimate is itself an underestimate. Though it is made in March 1984, it uses the exchange rate against the US dollar prevailing in June 1983, and the prices of September 1983. If up to date prices and exchange rates are used, the cost rises by a further £700 million – to around £9,400 million.[2]

Moreover, these estimates themselves exclude many large items of spending which form part of the total cost of the Trident programme. Funds needed for updating command and control systems, for example, include new 'Skynet' defence communications satellites now being built. Research is also underway on the vulnerability of UK satellites to new Soviet anti-satellite weapons.[3] The full extent of Trident-related spending on command and control systems is highly confidential information. Given the difficulty of communicating with submarines, however, it is likely to be considerable.

The Auditor-General's Report on the Trident project, published in February 1984, added two more items to the lengthening shopping list for Trident. First, the programme does not include the £250-£300 million for new production and research facilities at Aldermaston's Atomic Weapons Research Establishment. These facilities 'are required for purposes other than Trident but on which Trident in-service dates depend.' Second, £200 million of public funds is being spent on improvements to construction facilities at Vickers shipyards in Barrow in Furness, which will be used partly for Trident.[4]

The biggest missing item of all, however, is the *operating costs* of Trident. The cost of Britain's Polaris force in 1982-3 has been estimated at £1,050 million (at 1982-3 prices) – 7.4% of the total defence budget.[5] The much more sophisticated Trident system is likely to be at least as expensive to maintain and operate. Including its first 15 years of service – up to the year 2010 – Trident could cost £30,000 million at today's prices.

The escalating costs of Trident are a source of increasing worry even to its most fervent supporters. Anthony Cordesman, writing in *Armed Forces Journal International*, calculated that:

> There is a very good chance, based on past real escalation in US missile and British submarine and equipment costs, that the true program procurement cost (of Trident) will be 25 billion pounds, particularly if one adds in all the R&D related and 'minor' procurements that the UK has always ignored in publicly costing its strategic program.
>
> Remember too, that these figures cover only procurement. The true life cycle cost of the entire Trident force including submarines, C31, etc, from the mid 1980s – when major investment must begin – to the year 2000, will almost certainly be well in excess of 50 billion in 1983/84 pounds.

Accordingly, he concludes,

> Unfortunately, Britain probably cannot afford both guns and ballistic missiles.[6]

Even if Cordesman's figure proves to be a considerable overestimate, it may nevertheless prove nearer the truth than the official £8,700 million estimate.

Finally, the figures so far relate only to the cost of one component of Britain's nuclear weapons spending – the Trident programme. It excludes Polaris costs that will be incurred along with those for Trident until the last submarine is phased out in the late 1990s. Over the period from 1984 to the year 2000, Britain will have to pay for Polaris and Trident simultaneously. Moreover, the costs of Britain's 'tactical' and 'theatre' nuclear systems are also excluded from the above estimates. While less than those of the 'strategic' force, these will add a further additional burden.

British governments have traditionally been secretive on the costs of the nuclear force. Indeed the misplaced belief that nuclear weapons are an extremely cheap form of 'defence' is one of the main reasons for their continued popularity amongst some politicians. This belief is likely to come under severe challenge, however, over the next two or three years. By the late 1980s, the nuclear force will be costing about 15% of the total defence budget – £2,500 million (at 1984 prices) each year. The continued integration of tactical nuclear weapons into the armed forces will further add to the diversion of resources from conventional defences. As Lord Chalfont argued in 1980 (when the cost of Trident was 'only' £5000 million):

> The long-term effects of the decision taken in 1957 to base Britain's defence policy on an 'independent' nuclear deterrent have been seriously to impair our capacity for conventional military operations. The implications of the Trident decision are that this process will be intensified.[7]

The Coming Squeeze in Defence Spending

While Trident spending is now starting to build up, however, the *total* defence budget is likely to level off after 1985/6. Between 1978/9 and 1985/6, total defence spending is due to rise by 28.6% in real terms – 3.6% per annum.[8] Virtually none of this growth is attributable to Trident. In the late 1980s, however, unless there is a dramatic improvement in economic performance, defence spending will be subjected to an increasing squeeze. The government has already announced that it will not keep to the NATO target of 3% annual growth in defence spending after 1985/6. Indeed, in 1986-7, spending is at present planned to fall by 0.5% in real terms. And the Treasury appears likely to permit little, if any, significant growth in subsequent years.

This is still more than most government departments can expect. The reduction in defence spending's *rate of growth* is being accompanied by considerable further cuts in the *level* of spending in education, housing, transport, and local government. But the decrease in defence's growth rate is already leading to discussion of an impending budgetary crisis within the armed forces. The demand for more sophisticated, and expensive, weapons – conventional and nuclear – is now rising so fast that spending has to be increased each year simply to keep the numerical strength of the armed services constant. So the decrease in defence spending growth is bound to mean that either these ambitions are substantially curtailed or that the number of front line weapon systems – ships, aircraft, tanks, etc. – starts to decline sharply.

The advent of Trident will considerably increase this squeeze on the equipment budget. Spending on Trident could be as much as 20% of the defence equipment budget through the late 1980s and early 1990s.[9] As a result, spending on non-nuclear weapons will have to *fall* in real terms (see figure 5). Cuts in one or more of the three armed services' programmes will then be inevitable.

Figure 5:

The Military Cost of Trident

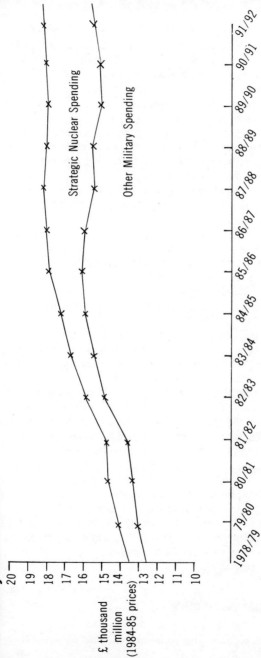

£ thousand million (1984-85 prices)

Strategic Nuclear Spending

Other Military Spending

Years 1978/9 to 1991/2

Notes: (i) 'Strategic nuclear spending' includes both Polaris and Trident.

(ii) 'Other military spending' includes spending on conventional and theatre nuclear forces.

The government has sought to play down the magnitude of this problem in two ways. Firstly, as we have seen already, it has under-estimated the total cost of Trident. Secondly, it has averaged Trident spending over the period 1980 to 1995 before calculating it as a percentage of the total defence budget. This has the effect of understating by a large margin the impact on the budget in the late 1980s and early 1990s.

Much of the military establishment has not been taken in by this doubtful arithmetic. Fearful of cuts in conventional forces, many prominent military figures, and increasing numbers of Conservative politicians, now favour the abandonment of Trident.

These concerns are also shared by Britain's allies. At a time when NATO commanders are pressing for increased conventional expenditures to 'raise the nuclear threshold', the need for Trident is widely questioned. This concern is likely to turn into outspoken hostility if, and when, the British have to cut their forces in Germany or the North Atlantic to pay for a nuclear programme widely seen elsewhere as an irrelevant status symbol.

Finally, the high import content of Trident spending makes it more vulnerable to cancellation. On official estimates around 50% of Trident costs will be on systems bought in the US, raising worries as to the effects on the balance of payments. The import content also considerably reduces the clout of the domestic lobby in favour of Trident especially when compared with the forces now pressing for an 'all-British' alternative.

With growing pressure from within the Conservative party, from the armed forces, and from NATO allies, there are now some reports that the government is actively considering the possibility of cancelling Trident and selecting a cheaper form of strategic nuclear force. If such a decision is to be taken, it will have to be taken relatively soon. Contracts are being signed and work started. Once the first submarine hull order (expected in 1985) is placed with Vickers, Barrow, committed expenditure will rise sharply. By 1988, according to government estimates, it expects to have spent or contractually committed about one third of the total cost (or £3,100 million at 1984/5 prices).[10] If a new government is elected in that year, the choice is likely to be between Trident and no strategic force at all.

A Cheaper Alternative

Many of those advocating cancellation of Trident, however, do believe that a British strategic nuclear force is needed. Their main concern with Trident is its exorbitant cost, and the effect that this will have on conventional defence programmes. Some of these critics – such as David Owen – argue that the lifetime of Polaris could be extended. The Chevaline programme, along with the £300 million spent on 100 new Polaris motors, means that the missiles will be able to operate at least until the year 2000. The submarines are likely to wear out in the mid 1990s, but they could be replaced by new submarines. There have even been suggestions that Polaris/Chevaline missiles could be 'cloned' onto the Trident submarines to be built at Barrow.

The most popular suggestion at present, however, is that Britain should replace Trident with its own force of cruise missiles. It is argued that Cruise would have several advantages. It is cheap – as little as £2 million per missile; it is much smaller than Trident and thus easier to conceal and move around; and new developments in technology – such as 'stealth' – promise to give Cruise a high rate of penetration to Soviet targets by the mid 1990s when Polaris needs to be replaced. The extensive US cruise missile development programme since 1980 has helped to increase the relative advantages that Cruise has over ballistic missiles such as Trident.

For Britain's Polaris replacement the two most favoured options at present are sea-launched cruise missiles (SLCMs) aboard submarines and air-launched cruise missiles (ALCMs) on aircraft. The third and cheapest possibility – ground-launched cruise missiles (GLCMs) – is ruled out because of vulnerability to pre-emptive attack.

Unlike the US GLCM force at Greenham Common, which would be used at a very early stage in a nuclear war, Britain's strategic force would need to be able to survive a first strike in order to fulfil its role as a second-strike 'deterrent'.

Sections of the Navy are particularly enthusiastic about SLCMs. Keith Speed MP, who was sacked as Navy Minister for his opposition to cuts in the surface fleet, has proposed putting US-made Tomahawk cruise missiles aboard 'hunter killer' submarines.[11] Recent reports suggest that the Admiralty Surface Weapons Establishment is now investigating the growing US experience with fitting SLCMs to its own nuclear-powered submarines in some detail.[12]

In the RAF there are some enthusiastic advocates for air-launched cruise missiles (ALCMs). These could be fitted on Tornado aircraft, which already have a 'theatre' nuclear role, in order to give them a capability for deep strikes into the Soviet Union.

Research is already underway into a 'long range stand-off air-to-ground missile carrying conventional munitions.'[13] It would be relatively straightforward to fit a nuclear warhead to these 'stand-off' missiles.

A further alternative that has been canvassed recently is a combination of air-launched cruise missiles with modified, multiple warhead, Pershing II missiles. The latter, it is argued, would 'have the ability to attack small military targets which Polaris cannot do' and 'could be operated in either a strategic or a theatre role.'[14] Feasibility studies on such a missile indicated that this proposal is entirely possible and could be produced within 5 years.

The list of possible alternatives to Trident is virtually endless. The basic point to be made, however, is clear. Although each of the main options would work out cheaper than Trident, and could therefore release funds for other purposes, none of them would be cheap. The submarine options – extending Polaris/Chevaline, SLCMs, or even going back to Trident I – would all require the construction of new boats specifically set aside for a strategic nuclear role. This would be a very expensive business: 52% of Trident D5's cost is on the submarines and their defensive ('tactical') weapons alone. One recent estimate calculates that a fleet of 5 SSCNs (cruise-missile-carrying submarines) would cost £4,000-£4,250 million at 1983 prices.[15]

Similar considerations apply to air-launched cruise missiles. Additional aircraft would have to be bought at a capital cost of between £2,500 million and £6,250 million.[16] The running costs of such a force are likely to considerably exceed that of a submarine force, and even that of Trident itself. A high proportion of crews, airfields, and support facilities would have to be kept on constant alert, ready to take off at a few minutes notice with nuclear missiles on board. Otherwise the Soviets could destroy Britain's strategic force in a pre-emptive attack. Finally, as the government argued in rejecting this option,

> Maintaining launch aircraft permanently airborne might seem to solve the problem of airfield vulnerability. But this is very expensive... Moreover, no British Government would want to have numerous nuclear-weapon carriers constantly airborne, year in and year out, in crowded airspace over and around our small country.[17]

The most widely canvassed alternatives do at least have the advantage that their contribution to the escalation in the arms race would be considerably less than the current Trident D5 programme. A retention of Polaris/Chevaline in new submarines would be the least escalatory option. Most of the other alternatives would, however, still present considerable problems. The modified Pershing II proposal would – like Trident D5 – be seen as giving Britain a 'decapitation' weapon; and, by being land-based, it would invite Soviet pre-emption. A cruise missile force would pose severe arms control problems since it would be impossible to distinguish it from conventionally-armed cruise missiles. Moreover, Cruise is likely to be as accurate, if not even more so, than Trident D5. With the development of stealth technology and supersonic propulsion systems, and the dual use of Cruise in nuclear and non-nuclear roles, a British cruise missile force would still increase Soviet fears of the vulnerability of their command, control and communications systems to a surprise attack.

Yet the arguments outlined in Chapter 4 on the questionable rationale for Trident D5 apply equally to these alternatives. For a force which has no military purpose, and may pose severe dangers, it is hard to see why *any* expenditure is justified on it. The search for cheaper alternatives to Trident is not only likely to yield relatively low financial returns. It is also misguided. The British government would be better to abandon its pretences to the status symbol of an 'independent deterrent' and divert the resources saved to economic reconstruction. It could then begin the process of re-orienting its armed forces towards a non-suicidal, and therefore non-nuclear, defence policy.

Trident Destroys Jobs

When every other argument has failed, advocates of increased arms spending resort to the jobs argument. Weapons like Trident are needed, they argue, in order to provide employment for those involved in producing them. Such a line of reasoning was implicit, for example, in Michael Heseltine's claim in 1983 that Labour's defence policy could lead to as many as 400,000 job losses.

These arguments are quite fallacious. Numerous studies have shown that money currently spent on arms, if spent on almost anything else, would create more jobs rather than fewer. Indeed a recent computer simulation has examined the effects of a 35% cut in British defence spending accompanied by an equivalent increase in public spending on health, education, roads, housing etc. It estimated that, while 250,000 jobs would be lost in defence, 350,000 jobs would be gained in the civilian sector.[18] Defence cuts would, therefore, actually lead to a net increase in employment.

Moreover, Trident, like many high technology defence projects, will be capital-intensive and skill-intensive. It will create relatively few jobs for each million pounds spent, and, since at least 45% of spending is to be in the United States, many of the jobs created will be in that country rather than in Britain.

If the government, nevertheless, decides to increase defence spending still further, and refuses to cancel Trident, it will impose a heavy burden on an increasingly fragile economy. Precisely those resources most needed for economic growth and international competitiveness are those used in substantial quantities in the arms industries. It is not entirely coincidental that those countries with the highest proportion of their national product devoted to the military – such as the US and the UK – are those with the lowest long-run rates of productivity growth (see figure 6). Nor that those countries with relatively low military spending – such as Japan – are able to devote the skills and talents of their people to producing a steadily rising standard of living.

Figures for net increase in employment, however important for the nation as a whole, may appear to be of limited relevance to those workers presently engaged, or soon to be engaged, on Trident contracts. For, understandably, it is their own jobs – not national statistics – that most directly concern them. And it must be recognised that cancellation of Trident, with no government provision for conversion or retraining, could have disastrous consequences for some individual workers. The key to solving this problem, however, is at hand in the skills of the workers involved. As a number of studies have shown, including 'Alternative work for Naval Shipbuilding Workers', published by the Vickers Shop Stewards Committee, there are alternatives. Skills currently wasted in producing weapons of mass destruction could instead be used for a large number of civilian products. There is no reason why, with a programme of planned conversion, the jobs of defence workers should not become more, rather than less, secure than at present.

Ironically, the straw that may break Trident's back is the growing unease in the armed services at its mounting cost. Fearful that conventional arms will be cut, many prominent military chiefs and Tory backbenchers are sceptical about Trident. The opposition appears to be most intense in the Navy, where it is seen as an obstacle to obtaining increased funds for a 'bluewater' surface fleet. As an article in *Navy International* argued recently:

Britain's current policy is to reduce expenditure on effective

Figure 6:
Guns or Butter

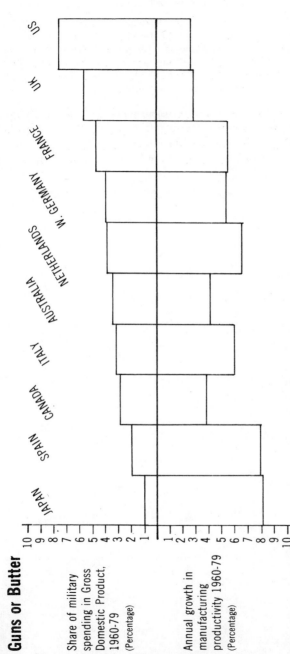

Share of military
spending in Gross
Domestic Product,
1960-79
(Percentage)

Annual growth in
manufacturing
productivity 1960-79
(Percentage)

JAPAN SPAIN CANADA ITALY AUSTRALIA NETHERLANDS W. GERMANY FRANCE UK US

Note: The countries shown have the ten largest, advanced capitalist economies.

Sources: Robert De Grasse, The Cost and Consequences of Reagan's Military Build-up, pp. 50-2 (New York, Council on Economic Priorities, 1982); SIPRI Yearbook (London, Taylor and Francis, various years); OECD Main Economic Indicators, (World Bank); World Development Report (London, Oxford University Press, various years).

conventional forces, whilst overspending on the almost valueless strategic nuclear arm. The overall result is rather contrary to Conservative party claims. Removal of the strategic forces of our country would not cut jobs if money was diverted to a serious programme of shipbuilding. Rather, more jobs would be created in the hard pressed shipbuilding and aircraft industries.[19]

Trident's fate, under the Conservatives at any rate, may hang on whether Mrs. Thatcher's sense of imperial grandeur appears to be more gratified by a nuclear force that can never be used, or by a force to fight very real wars in the South Atlantic or the Persian Gulf.

Chapter Six
Trident and Disarmament

Perhaps the most bogus argument of all for Trident, however, is that it is needed to enable the British government to 'negotiate from strength'. The government claims to be committed to 'multilateral disarmament', but opposed to 'unilateral disarmament'. For how can we get the Soviets to give up their weapons if we give ours up first? As the 1983 Defence White Paper argued in criticising 'one-sided measures':

> The policy of maintaining adequate defences while being willing to negotiate balanced reductions in the forces of both sides has brought the Soviet Union to the negotiating table in Geneva. To abandon it now in favour of untried and potentially dangerous alternatives would be to put the security of this country and our allies at risk.[1]

This professed support of 'multilateral disarmament', however, is in reality little more than a public relations exercise hiding the true situation – a massive build up in Britain's nuclear stockpile. The hypocrisy of the government's 'multilateral' policy is seen most clearly in its refusal to allow Britain's nuclear weapons even to be *counted* in recent disarmament negotiations. It has rejected Soviet proposals to include Polaris, and in future Trident, in the now suspended INF talks because these are strategic forces. Yet it has also rejected their inclusion in the strategic arms limitation talks because they are not American.

Indeed Britain's refusal even to count its strategic nuclear force was a major reason for the failure of the Geneva talks on Intermediate Nuclear Forces (INF) in 1983. In January 1983, Soviet leader Yuri Andropov made a number of significant concessions in the negotiations, offering to reduce the number of SS20s in Europe to 162 – equivalent to the total UK (64) and French (98) strategic nuclear missiles. In May 1983, he went further and offered equivalence in warhead numbers between the triple-warhead SS20s and the British and French forces. This would have meant a reduction in SS20 numbers in Europe to 140 and the dismantling of around 100 SS20 missiles and their warheads. As a result of British and French intransigence, these moves proved fruitless. In December 1983 the first ground-launched cruise missiles were deployed at Greenham Common air base in Berkshire, and the Soviet Union withdrew from the talks.

There would have been some logic in Britain's refusal to count Polaris/Trident in the INF talks if, instead, it had agreed to include them in the strategic arms talks (START). Yet the government has rejected this alternative too. It argues that:

> The UK's strategic deterrent force cannot feature in these negotiations, which are bilateral between the two superpowers and concern their strategic forces alone. In any event, the British deterrent represents only a very small proportion of the strategic forces of the US or the Soviet Union, and is of a minimum size compatible with ensuring a cost-effective deterrent at all times. This will remain the case with Trident as it is with Polaris now.[2]

This argument is entirely inadequate. It does not explain how Trident can be a 'minimum size' nuclear force when it can destroy between 8 and 14 times as many targets as the current 'minimum deterrent', Polaris. It fails to recognize that, if deployed, Trident will have considerably more than a 'very small proportion' of the superpower warhead count. On present SALT counting rules, a MIRVed missile is assumed to carry the maximum number of warheads possible at all times, whether or not it actually does so. If these rules remain unchanged, therefore, the UK Trident D5 force will be considered to have 896 warheads even if the government sticks to its intention only to deploy the number previously planned for the C4. Together with the French nuclear force, there will then be as many as 2000 strategic nuclear warheads in the possession of countries not included in the bilateral US-Soviet arms talks. These cannot seriously be described as a 'very small proportion' of the Soviet Union's current strategic arsenal of 8100 warheads. Any agreement on substantial cuts in the size of superpower forces is even more unlikely if the forces of US allies – such as Britain – are able to expand without restriction.

In practical terms, it is difficult to believe that future arms control agreements can be reached between the superpowers except on the basis of the principle of rough *parity*. Given the vast overkill that exists in current arsenals, the attachment to this principle may have little rational foundation. Nevertheless it exists. The Soviet Union appears to be unwilling to accept a situation where its nuclear forces are numerically clearly 'inferior' to those of its NATO rivals. In turn no US President could hope to win political support for an agreement that allowed the Soviets more strategic weapons than the US. These two, rather different, requirements proved to be compatible in the negotiations for SALT 1 and SALT II, largely because of the relatively small British and French arsenals at the time. When 'third parties' have 2000 warheads between them, however, it would make any further strategic arms agreement impossible unless one of the superpowers abandoned the concept of 'parity'. Having helped to ensure the failure of the 'theatre' nuclear talks by its refusal to count Polaris missiles in 1983, Britain now appears set on wrecking future 'strategic' negotiations by its determination to press ahead with Trident. It is a heavy price to pay for 'negotiation from strength'.

Bombs for All

The Trident decision will also damage the attempts to control the spread of nuclear weapons. It is difficult to see how the decision is consistent with Britain's pledge, in Article VI of the 1968 Non-Proliferation Treaty:

> Each of the Parties to the Treaty undertakes to pursue negotiations in good faith on effective measures relating to cessation of the nuclear arms race at an early date and to nuclear disarmament, and on a treaty on general and complete disarmament under strict and effective international control.[3]

Moreover, the example of Britain's expanding nuclear arsenal is unlikely to be entirely unnoticed by the leaders of the world's near-nuclear states. Britain faces no immediate threat to its national survival. It has not been invaded for almost three centuries. It has a close military alliance with its immediate neighbours and with the US. Compared with the vast majority of states that exist today, therefore, Britain has less reason for requiring the protection which, it is argued, a national nuclear force provides. Yet its government is now planning to considerably increase the power of its 'deterrent' as a safeguard against improbable contingencies that may occur in the early part of the 21st century.

With Britain acting in this way, why should other countries continue to deny themselves a capability which is clearly valued very highly? New states, with precarious governments and frequent threats to their very existence, are in abundance in today's world: Israel, South Africa, Pakistan, South Korea and Taiwan are only some of the more obvious examples. If they followed the British government's arguments, all these countries would be more secure if they too had their own nuclear force.

The technical constraints on any industrialised or semi-industrialised country acquiring a small force of nuclear weapons are now rapidly diminishing. For as many as 30-40 states, it is mainly political constraints – pressure from the superpowers, adherence to the NPT, fear of provoking an arms race – that are holding them back. Yet once these constraints start dissolving, perhaps because of a public declaration by a nearby state that it has acquired its own 'A'-bomb or perhaps because of the use of nuclear blackmail by a superpower, proliferation could accelerate dramatically. The states in areas of recent or ongoing conflict are likely to be first: Israel, Libya, Iran, Iraq, South Korea, Pakistan, India, Argentina, South Africa. Indeed some of these states have had a capability to make a nuclear weapon quickly for some years, while at the same time, it appears, not actually doing so. Once those states went openly nuclear, the rush would no doubt start in earnest. Japan, Australia, Egypt and Brazil all have the technical capability to acquire primitive nuclear weapons, and would probably do so. European countries – Spain, Italy, Greece and Turkey – might feel forced to follow suit were North African powers such as Libya to 'go nuclear'. With as many as 30 nuclear weapons states, who can doubt that, sooner rather than later, the moratorium on their use that has existed since 1945 would be broken.

Renunciation of Trident by Britain cannot stem this process by itself. It can, however, make some contribution to influencing leaders in near-nuclear countries. The demonstration that the existing nuclear powers were at last making some progress towards disarmament could have a considerable restraining effect on them. This effect could only be reinforced if one of those nuclear powers were willing to give up its 'independent' nuclear force altogether.

Towards a Sensible Defence Policy

Cancellation of Trident would not only contribute to a superpower arms limitation agreement and restrain the proliferation of nuclear weapons. It could also be a positive first step towards establishing a sensible defence policy for Britain and indeed for NATO as a whole. There is strong pressure in both Western Europe and the US for a radical reduction in reliance on nuclear weapons. In Europe, the new peace movements have already persuaded many left-of-centre parties to adopt more radical policies on defence. In eight out of 10 of NATO's European democracies, the major left-wing party was opposed to Cruise and Pershing II deployment in December 1983. Only the French and Portuguese socialists – who refuse to station any foreign nuclear weapons on their own soil – supported the US decision to go ahead.

Nor is the opposition to the current arms build-up confined to the European socialist parties. Several centrist parties – such as the British Liberals and Dutch Christian Democrats – contain strong anti-nuclear factions. The new Green parties, particularly strong in West Germany, have made opposition to all nuclear weapons central to their campaigning. In the US the peace movement has also made considerable progress in a short period of time with the 'freeze' proposal now supported by most Democratic politicians, including all the candidates for the Presidential nomination. A growing number of military officers favour a radical reappraisal of current defence policy. A British government that cancelled Trident and committed itself to a non-nuclear defence policy could tip the scales decisively in this debate.

Some critics suggest that British nuclear disarmament would have little influence on the global arms race between the superpowers. This argument is unduly dismissive of Britain's current role in NATO. Britain has a sophisticated force of strategic and tactical weapons and a key role as an 'unsinkable aircraft carrier' in US plans for limited nuclear war in Europe. Were Britain to scrap its own nuclear weapons – strategic and tactical – and ask the US to remove its nuclear bases from the UK, it would, at a minimum, require a major rethink of NATO defence policy. Were a non-nuclear policy also to be supported in West Germany and the Low countries, NATO policy could be revolutionised.

In particular Britain could argue that, in parallel with independent British nuclear disarmament, NATO itself should move towards a non-nuclear defence. It could begin this process by removing all battlefield nuclear weapons and adopting a policy of No First Use of nuclear weapons. Such a policy would transform the psychological climate in the armed forces. It would rule out entirely the use of nuclear weapons to avert conventional defeat; and it would therefore force the military to think about, and plan for, a credible non-nuclear defence for NATO. Together with the removal of all the nuclear weapons associated with First Use – including all the vulnerable landbased missiles – it would be a major step towards a non-nuclear policy.

A No First Use *policy* would also remove the West's objections to Soviet proposals for a European nuclear-weapon-free zone. In the past, NATO has insisted on stationing nuclear weapons in Europe as a deterrent against a Soviet invasion with conventional forces. Once No First Use were adopted, such an argument would no longer apply. Theatre nuclear weapons – such as cruise and Pershing II missiles, Tornado and F111 aircraft, and nuclear artillery shells – would have no purpose. Support for negotiations on a Nuclear Free Zone in Europe would follow naturally from a No First Use policy; and would in turn be an important step towards the removal of the armies of the two superpowers from Europe altogether.

Proposals by Britain for such a NATO policy cannot, of course, be guaranteed success. It would face opposition from several, perhaps most, of the other NATO members. Were a No First Use policy to be rejected by NATO as a whole, Britain would have no alternative other than to withdraw its conventional forces from Europe. It would not be possible for Britain's 55,000 strong army in Germany to follow a non-nuclear defence policy if the US Army and German Bundeswehr were still committed to the suicidal 'flexible response' strategy. The government would have to abandon its non-nuclear policy or disengage from NATO.

Such a choice, however, may not be necessary. The insanity of current policy is becoming increasingly obvious in most Western European countries. Provided that the British government were both determined and united, it may find that it is pushing at an open door. If the Soviet Union were sensible enough to respond to NATO initiatives, moreover, the process could be carried forward at a surprisingly rapid pace towards a more far-reaching relaxation of tension in Europe.

A Freeze Now

Independent – or 'unilateral' – disarmament initiatives by Britain would have their greatest effect in Europe. But Britain could – and should – also use its position to press for a *freeze* on the strategic nuclear arsenals of the two superpowers. Such a freeze is the main proposal of the US peace movement, and has been supported (in principle at least) by both the Soviet government and by Walter Mondale, the Democrats' Presidential candidate in November 1984. It would stop the production of fissionable material for nuclear weapons, the production, testing and deployment of warheads and missiles, and the deployment of additional nuclear bombers. It would thus stop the deployment of the new generation of highly accurate 'counterforce' weapons – such as Trident D5. If such an agreement were reached, putting a lid on superpower nuclear arsenals and thus *halting* the arms race, it would then be possible to negotiate 'deep cuts', thus at long last *reversing* the arms race.

The two superpowers would still be likely to retain considerable 'second strike' forces for some time. A successful freeze agreement, however, if combined with Nuclear-Weapons-Free Zones in Europe and elsewhere, could create a climate for moving to a 'minimum deterrent' policy. Each superpower would retain only enough nuclear weapons – probably in relatively invulnerable submarines – to be able to destroy the other's cities once over. Two forces of 400-500 warheads (at most) would be needed for this purpose, as against the 55,000 warheads currently in the possession of the superpowers. It may then be possible to agree to the establishment of the international control bodies which will be necessary if a comprehensive disarmament agreement is to be reached.

Were such a process to be started, it might also offer a constructive role for some of the British scientists at Aldermaston displaced by Trident cancellation. They could be redeployed into advising the UN and the international community on technical aspects of arms control. In the past, Soviet reluctance to allow on-site verification has, on several occasions, been used by the US as a pretext to block genuine disarmament proposals. Nevertheless, the reality is that some verification of agreements is necessary if trust is to be developed sufficiently for genuine disarmament to take place. Britain's considerable expertise in nuclear weapons could be profitably employed in this field to great effect, exposing fallacious arguments and suggesting new remedies. It would be a powerful symbol of the potential for turning 'swords into ploughshares', and of the new role for Britain in the world which nuclear disarmament would involve.

Conclusion

The Trident D5 programme is both dangerous and wasteful. It is imperative that it be cancelled. It should be rejected, however, not only for these negative reasons, but also because cancellation would provide an opportunity for Britain to make a contribution to reversing the arms race both in Europe and globally. Massive unease already exists, even within traditionally pro-nuclear governments, on the extent to which our future has been 'mortgaged to the nuclear response.' Current 'defence' policy is widely recognized as bankrupt and increasingly dangerous. What is so far lacking is a government willing to propose a clear alternative policy. By proposing a credible, non-nuclear, defence policy, and supporting genuine arms control initiatives, a disarmament-orientated

British government could act as a catalyst for wide-ranging changes.

It is possible that, if Britain's nuclear force was phased out gradually on grounds of cost alone – for example, by allowing Polaris to 'die a natural death' in the 1990s – nuclear disarmament might simply be seen as symptomatic of Britain's declining economic status. If a UK government, on the other hand, were to take the decision to disarm the strategic nuclear force as a positive act of policy, the political consequences would be considerable. Such a step could have a catalytic effect on opinion in other NATO members – including the US – and thus force a major rethink in NATO's current defence policies.

The obstacles which exist to a process of effective disarmament are considerable. They are not, however, insurmountable. In four short years, the pro-nuclear establishment has seen the carefully constructed intellectual apparatus of 'deterrence' exposed as suicidal nonsense. The people of Europe and the world now have a unique chance – perhaps a last chance – to stop the arms race and move towards a more secure future. We can start that process here in Britain by cancelling Trident and adopting a non-nuclear defence policy. The arms race **can** be stopped.

Notes

1. Introduction

1. Gallup opinion poll conducted from 23 to 28 May 1984. When asked 'Do you approve or disapprove of the British Government's decision to spend ten billion pounds on the new Trident nuclear missile submarine?', 28 per cent approved, 63 per cent disapproved, and 9 per cent didn't know. (Reported in *Campaign*, July 1984).
2. *Statement on the Defence Estimates, 1982*, Cmnd. 8529, p.6. (London, HMSO, 1982).
3. *House of Lords Debate*, December 18, 1979, col. 1628.

2. Britain and the Bomb

1. Margaret Gowing, *Independence and Deterrence: Britain and Atomic Energy 1945-1952*, p. 407. (London, Macmillan, 1974).
2. cited in *Ibid*. pp. 202-203.
3. cited in *Ibid*. p. 229.
4. *Ibid*. pp. 232-233.
5. Andrew Pierre, *Nuclear Politics: The British Experience With An Independent Strategic Force 1939-1970*, pp. 86-90. (London, Oxford University Press, 1972).
6. *The Times*, February 24, 1958.
7. C.J. Bartlett, *A History of Postwar Britain 1945-74*, p. 156. (London, Longmans, 1977).
8. John Simpson, *The Independent Nuclear State: The United States, Britain and the Military Atom*, p. 255. (London, Macmillan, 1983). Joseph Gallacher, *Nuclear stocktaking: a count of Britain's warheads* (University of Lancaster, 1982).
9. Paul Bracken, *The Command and Control of Nuclear Forces*, p. 164. (London, Yale University Press, 1983).
10. Paul Rogers, *Guide to Nuclear Weapons 1984-85*, pp. 73-74 (Bradford School of Peace Studies, 1984).
11. There have been unconfirmed reports that those Polaris missiles now fitted with *Chevaline* may have only two warheads.
12. The Nassau Agreement is quoted in full in Andrew Pierre, *op. cit.* pp. 346-347.

13. The government has estimated the total cost of *Chevaline* at £1000 million (see *Ninth Report from the Committee of Public Accounts, 'Chevaline* Improvement to the Polaris Missile System', (London, HMSO, 1982), p. 1). This figure, however, is calculated on a confusing amalgam of current and constant prices. Converted into constant September 1984 prices it is equivalent to £2200 million. For an estimate of total Polaris costs see *Fourth Report from the Defence Committee*, 'Strategic Nuclear Weapons Policy' p. 229. (London, HMSO, 1981).

14. Lawrence Freedman, *Britain and Nuclear Weapons*, pp. 53-54. (London, Macmillan, 1980).

3. The Choice of Trident

1. 'The Future United Kingdom Strategic Nuclear Deterrent Force', *Defence Open Government Document 80/23*. p. 25. (London, HMSO, 1980).

2. J.J. Tritten, 'The Trident System: Submarines, Missiles and Strategic Doctrine', *Naval War College Review*, p. 67. Jan/Feb 1983.

3. 'The United Kingdom Trident Programme', *Defence Open Government Document 82/1*, (London, HMSO, 1982).

4. 'Strategic Nuclear Weapons Policy', *First Special Report from the Defence Committee*, HC266 (1981-82) p. 2.

5. *Ibid*. p. 3.

6. *Defense Daily*, January 25, 1983.

7. *First Special Report from the Defence Committee, op cit*. p. 24.

8. Ian Smart, *The Future of the British Nuclear Deterrent: Technical, Economic and Strategic Issues,* p. 28. (London, RIIA, 1977).

9. *The Observer*, September 12, 1982.

10. Lawrence Freedman, *op. cit*., p. xiii. Also see Air Chief Marshal Sir John Barraclough, 'Britain's Strategic Nuclear Deterrent', *NATO's Fifteen Nations*, Feb/March 1982.

11. Geoffrey Kemp, *Nuclear Forces for Medium Powers*, note 25. (London, IISS, 1974).

12. *Fourth Report from the Defence Committee, op. cit*. p. 80.

13. 'The United Kingdom Trident Programme', *op. cit*. p. 6.

14. Paul Rogers, *Guide to Nuclear Weapons 1984-85*, p. 113. (Bradford School of Peace Studies, 1984).

15. George Crossley, *Disarmament Negotiations: The Way Forward*, p. 17, (London, CND Publications, 1984).

16. Paul Bracken, *op. cit.* p. 234.
17. Owen Greene, *Europe's Folly: The Facts and Arguments about Cruise*, p. 74. (London, CND Publications, 1983).
18. *Los Angeles Times*, May 22, 1983.
19. Paul Bracken, *op. cit.* p. 229.
20. 'Ministry of Defence: Trident Project', *Report by the Comptroller and Auditor General*, p. 1, (London, HMSO, 1984).
21. *The Guardian*, May 22, 1984.
22. *Statement on the Defence Estimates 1983*, Cmnd. 8951-1, p. 7. (London, HMSO, 1983).
23. Andrew Pierre, *op. cit.* p. 227.
24. *The Economist*, March 3, 1984.
25. 'Trident II', *Maritime Defence*, January, 1983.
26. *The Economist*, January 14, 1984.
27. *Los Angeles Times*, May 24, 1983.
28. *Pittsburgh Press*, December 8, 1982.

4. Trident: What Is It For?

1. Colin S. Gray and Keith Payne, 'Victory is Possible', *Foreign Policy*, Summer 1980, 39, pp. 18-27.
2. 'The United Kingdom Trident Programme', *op. cit.* p. 6.
3. 'The Future United Kingdom Strategic Nuclear Deterrent Force', *op. cit.* p. 6.
4. *Fourth Report from the Defence Committee, op. cit.* p. 85.
5. Graeme Auton, 'Nuclear Deterrence and the Medium Power: A Proposal for Doctrinal Change in the British and French Cases', *Orbis*, Summer 1976, p. 377.
6. For a critique of this assumption, see Desmond Ball, *Can Nuclear War be Controlled?*, (London, International Institute for Strategic Studies, 1981).
7. Geoffrey Kemp, *op. cit.*, p. 176.
8. David Hobbs, *Alternatives to Trident*, p. 7, (Aberdeen Studies in Defence Economics, Summer 1983).
9. Julian Critchley, 'Trident's Potential Targets', *Royal United Services Institute Journal*, pp. 41-42. March 1984.
10. 'The Future United Kingdom Strategic Nuclear Deterrent Forces', *op. cit.* p. 5.
11. *Ibid.* pp. 3-4.
12. Foreword to 'The United Kingdom Trident Programme', *op. cit.*
13. See, for example, Alan Clark, MP, 'Founding Fortress Britain', *The Guardian*, February 15, 1982.

14. Daniel Ellsberg, 'Call to Mutiny', *END Papers One*, Winter 1981-82.
15. Phillip Darby, *British Defence Policy East of Suez*, pp. 120-121, (London, Oxford University Press, 1973).
16. Andrew Pierre, *op. cit.* pp. 284-287.
17. Tam Dalyell, *Thatcher's Torpedo*, (London, Cecil Woolf, 1983), pp. 32-33.
18. *House of Commons*, July 19, 1983, cols. 214-220.
19. *House of Commons*, November 4, 1982, cols. 206-214.
20. Neville Brown, 'The Future of the British Deterrent: 1. The Use of Nuclear Weapons', *Navy International*, April 1983, p. 244.
21. Cited in Lawrence Freedman, *op. cit.* p. 136.
22. *First Special Report from the Defence Committee, op. cit.* p.21.
23. Seymour Hersh, *The Price of Power*, (New York Summit Books, 1983), pp. 128-131 and *passim*.
24. 'The Future United Kingdom Strategic Nuclear Deterrent Force', *op. cit.* p.5.
25. *The Times*, May 16, 1980.

5. The Costs

1. *House of Commons*, March 13, 1984, col. 263-4.
2. 'Statement on the Defence Estimates 1984', *First Report from the Defence Committee*, HC436 (1983-84), pp. xvii-xviii, (London, HMSO, 1984).
3. *First Special Report from the Defence Committee, op. cit*, p.6.
4. *Report by the Comptroller and Auditor General, op. cit.* p. 2.
5. David Greenwood, 'Economic Constraints and Political Preferences', in John Baylis (ed.) *Alternative Approaches to British Defence Policy*, p. 34, (London, Macmillan, 1983).
6. Anthony Cordesman, 'British Defense: A Time for Hard Choices', *Armed Forces Journal International*, September 1983, pp. 58, 68, 114.
7. *The Times*, August 4, 1980.
8. *House of Commons*, March 13, 1984, (*Written Answer*), cols. 77-78.
9. See *House of Commons*, June 18, 1984, cols. 64-65; and David Greenwood, *Trident: The Budgetary Impact*, (Aberdeen, mimeo, 1984). The proportion of the equipment budget which Trident will take is a subject of intense debate. One of the major sources of contention is the exact definition

of 'equipment spending'. On the UK Government's definition, equipment spending was 46.2% of the total 1983/4 defence budget. On the narrower definition used by NATO (which excludes minor items and spares), equipment spending was only 28.2% of the British defence budget in the same year. Trident spending will thus be 14-16% of total equipment spending at its peak in 1988-92 (using the UK government definition), or 24-27% (using the NATO definition).

10. *House of Commons*, November 29, 1983, (Written Answer), col. 480.
11. *The Guardian*, March 12, 1982.
12. *Evening Standard*, May 9, 1984.
13. *Statement on the Defence Estimates 1983, op. cit.* p. 13.
14. Air Vice-Marshal Stewart Menaul, *Alternatives to Trident*, pp. 7-8. (London, Foreign Affairs Research Institute, 1982).
15. David Hobbs, *op. cit.* p. 61.
16. *Ibid*.
17. 'The Future United Kingdom Strategic Nuclear Deterrent Force', *op. cit.* p. 11.
18. J.P. Dunne and R.P. Smith, *The Economic Consequences of Reduced UK Military Expenditure*, (London, Birkbeck College, 1983).
19. Ian Simpson and M.G. Davey, 'A Valueless Deterrent?', *Navy International*, pp. 699-700, November 1983.

6. Trident and Disarmament

1. *Statement on the Defence Estimates 1983, op. cit.* p. 9.
2. *Statement on the Defence Estimates 1982*, Cmnd 8529-1, p. 7, (London, HMSO, 1982).
3. See *Nature*, April 12, 1984.

Guide to Further Reading

For study of all aspects of **Britain's defence policy**, the annual *Statement on the Defence Estimates* is a valuable source. So too are the reports of the *House of Commons Defence Committee*. On the Trident decision itself, the two 'Open Government Documents' (*The Future United Kingdom Strategic Nuclear Deterrent Force* (1980) and *The United Kingdom Trident Programme* (1982)) are also useful.

On the **history of Britain's nuclear weapons policy**, the most comprehensive account is Andrew Pierre, *Nuclear Politics. The British Experience with an Independent Strategic Force, 1939-70* (London, Oxford University Press, 1972). For the years from 1939 to 1952, Margaret Gowing's work remains an unsurpassed account: in 3 volumes, *Britain and Atomic Energy, 1939-45; Brittain and Atomic Energy 1945-52*, Vols 1 and 2 (published Macmillan, 1964 and 1974). For an informative account of the technical evolution of the British Bomb, see John Simpson, *The Independent Nuclear State: The United States, Britain and the Military Atom*, (London, Macmillan, 1983).

The most thorough and authoritative study of the **nuclear arms race** is probably Gwyn Prins (ed.), *Defended to Death*, (London, Penguin, 1983). On the dangers which the new generation of 'counterforce' nuclear weapons pose, see Malcolm Dando and Paul Rogers, *The Death of Deterrence*, (London, CND Publications, 1984). For a comprehensive, and unique, compilation of information on the world's nuclear arsenals, see Paul Rogers, *Guide to Nuclear Weapons 1984-85*, (Bradford, Peace Studies, 1984). And for a powerful exposure of the extent of the United States military presence in the UK, see Duncan Campbell, *The Unsinkable Aircraft Carrier*, (London, Michael Joseph, 1984).

On the **economic costs of the military**, see Mary Kaldor, *The Baroque Arsenal*, (London, Andre Deutsch, 1982); Dan Smith and Ron Smith, *The Economics of Militarism* (London, Pluto, 1983).

Finally, those interested in the **alternatives** to reliance on nuclear weapons will find *Defence without the Bomb: the Report of the Alternative Defence Commission* (London, Taylor and Francis, 1983) invaluable.

Glossary

ABM
: Anti-ballistic Missile. A missile designed to intercept and destroy an incoming warhead from a ballistic missile.

ALCM
: Air-launched Cruise Missile.

ASW
: Anti-submarine Warfare.

B52
: United States intercontinental range bomber. Now being equipped with ALCM's.

Ballistic missile
: A missile, the propulsion for which is terminated a few minutes after launch. It then follows an elliptical trajectory caused by gravity and aerodynamic drag.

Battlefield nuclear weapon
: A nuclear weapon used in direct military combat on land.

Chevaline
: A programme to redesign the 'front-end' of the UK's Polaris missiles. It involves the inclusion of a number of decoys in the re-entry system and the manoeuvring of the entire missile front-end before release of the various re-entry vehicles. Chevaline appears to have either two or three warheads, but it is not a MIRV system. It should be fitted in all four Polaris submarines by 1988.

Chief of Defence Staff
: The most senior officer in Britain's armed forces. Responsible for advising the Secretary of State for Defence on policy, strategy and related matters.

Conventional war
: A war in which no nuclear (or chemical or biological) weapons have been used.

Controlled escalation
: The central concept in US and NATO nuclear policy. It calls for the capability to contain (or win) a conflict at any level, and to escalate the conflict in a 'controlled' manner (by use of nuclear weapons if 'necessary').

Counterforce attack
: An attack directed against targets of military significance, such as the opponent's nuclear forces, radar stations, airfields, barracks, and weapons stores.

Countervalue attack
An attack directed against civilian targets such as cities and industrial areas.

Cruise missile
A pilotless guided aircraft, which relies on continuous propulsion throughout its flight. It can be launched from ground, sea or air and delivers a conventional, chemical or nuclear warhead with great accuracy.

Decapitation attack
An attack directed against the facilities for command and control of an opponent's nuclear forces. Designed to prevent any order being given to retaliate.

Disarming first strike
A sudden pre-emptive attack on an adversary's military, particularly nuclear, forces, designed to destroy its ability to retaliate. In practice, it may seek only to leave the adversary with insufficient nuclear weapons to inflict more than 'acceptable' damage – however that may be defined.

Dual capable
Weapons which are capable of being used in both nuclear and conventional roles.

EMP
Electromagnetic Pulse. An extremely powerful voltage pulse that is generated by nuclear explosions. It can destroy or damage sensitive electrical equipment such as radar, microchips, and communications lines over a wide area. A large (10Mt) explosion 200 miles above the US, for example, would affect the whole of North America.

F111
US LRTNF nuclear bomber aircraft with combat range of 1800 km. 150 currently stationed at Lakenheath and Upper Heyford in England. Each can carry up to three nuclear warheads.

First strike
A pre-emptive attack on an adversary's military facilities: *see Disarming first strike*.

Flexible response
NATO's official strategy since 1967. It calls for preparations which assume that a nuclear war in Europe can be kept limited. It declares that NATO might choose to use nuclear weapons in response to a conventional attack. It is closely linked to the concept of *controlled escalation*.

GLCM	Ground Launched Cruise Missile. This is the version of cruise missile which NATO is now deploying in Western Europe. 96 in total are due to be stationed at Greenham Common, Berkshire. A further 64 are planned for Molesworth in Cambridgeshire before the end of 1986.
Harden	Reduce the vulnerability of a target by shielding it (for example, by constructing a silo or bunker).
ICBM	Intercontinental ballistic missile, with a range of over 3700 miles.
INF	Intermediate range Nuclear Forces; those with a range of between 1000 and 3700 miles.
Kiloton (Kt)	The explosive equivalent to one thousand tons of TNT. The atomic bomb which destroyed Hiroshima in 1945 had an explosive power of 12.5 kilotons.
Launch on Warning	A system by which missiles are launched in retaliation for a perceived nuclear attack even before warheads have exploded.
MRV	Multiple Re-entry Vehicles. A missile which carries several *re-entry vehicles* which are all directed against the same target.
MIRV	Multiple Independently-targetable Re-entry Vehicles. A missile which carries several *re-entry vehicles* each of which is capable of being directed against separate targets long distances apart.
MX Missile	US land-based ICBM due to be deployed in the late 1980s. Re-named the 'Peacekeeper' by President Reagan.
Megaton (Mt)	Explosive equivalent to one million tons of TNT. (see *kiloton*).
'Minimum deterrent'	A nuclear force sufficient only to inflict unacceptable damage on an opponent after a surprise attack. Currently both the United States and the Soviet Union have many more nuclear weapons than are required for a minimum deterrent.

Minuteman II	US ICBM with single warhead rated at 1.5 megatons. 550 are currently in service.
Minuteman III	US ICBM with three warheads, each rated at 170 kilotons. Currently being modernised with the addition of the Mark-12a warhead, which has increased accuracy and is rated at 335 kilotons.
NATO	North Atlantic Treaty Organisation. A military alliance between the US and some West European countries established in 1949.
No First Use	A policy which prohibits the use of nuclear weapons, except in retaliation to their use by an opponent. If adopted, such a policy would lead to drastic cuts in nuclear arsenals. It runs directly in opposition to current NATO policy. (See *flexible response*).
Nuclear Winter	The severe effects of a large-scale nuclear war on the earth's atmosphere and climate. Recent studies suggest that such a war would result in the blocking out of the sun by soot and dust for a prolonged period – affecting the 'victor' as much as the vanquished.
Pershing II	US missile with a range of at least 1000 miles and an accuracy of tens of yards. Targets in the USSR could be destroyed ten minutes after launching from locations in West Germany and Alaska.
Polaris	SLBM which carries three MRVs of 200 kilotons. Now withdrawn from service in the US Navy. The UK has 64 Polaris missiles aboard four submarines. These are currently being updated with *Chevaline*.
Poseidon	US SLBM. There are currently 304 Poseidon missiles in service, each of which can carry up to 14 40-kiloton MIRVed warheads.
Pre-delegation	The delegation of authority for ordering the launch of nuclear weapons from political leaders to military subordinates.
(1984) prices	The cost of an item or programme expressed in the price of a particular base year (1973, 1984, etc.) In order to accurately compare the

	cost of two items, it is necessary to ensure that they both use the same base year.
Real terms	The cost of an item or programme after allowing for the effects of inflation. Calculated by adjusting the actual, or estimated, money cost to the prices of a particular base year (see previous entry).
Re-entry vehicle	A vehicle carried on a *ballistic missile* which is released once the missile leaves the earth's atmosphere. Each carries a single *warhead*, which is usually able to follow a trajectory towards a separate target. (See *MIRV*). Some older missiles carry several re-entry vehicles which cannot be separately targetted (see *MRV*).
SALT	Strategic Arms Limitation Talks between the US and USSR which began in 1969.
Second strike	The use of nuclear weapons in response to an enemy's first strike.
Silo	Underground missile shelter, usually protected by reinforced concrete and a massive steel cap which has to be raised before the missile is launched.
SIOP	Single Integrated Operational Plan. The US plan for the conduct of nuclear war. The current version lists over 40,000 potential targets.
SLBM	Submarine Launched Ballistic Missile.
SLCM	Sea Launched Cruise Missile: launched from submarines and surface ships. The US Navy intends to install over 4000 SLCMs during the 1980s in several different versions. They are externally indistinguishable, and it is not known which ships will carry the nuclear-armed version. Deployment in surface ships and submarines has now begun.
SS20	Mobile Soviet intermediate range missile. First deployed in 1977, each missile carries three independently targetable warheads rated at 150 kilotons. An estimated 378 are now deployed, 270 of which are within range of Western Europe.

START	Strategic Arms Reduction Talks between the US and USSR. Started in November 1981 following the non-ratification of SALT II by the US Senate. Suspended since the initial deployment of Cruise and Pershing II missiles in Western Europe in December, 1983.
Stealth technology	Design techniques that makes cruise missiles and aircraft hard to detect by radar or other means.
Strategic nuclear weapons	Weapons capable of reaching an adversary's homeland.
Tactical nuclear weapons	Nuclear weapons intended for use in immediate support of a military operation.
Theatre nuclear weapons	Weapons of varying ranges that are intended for use in a particular 'theatre' (geographical area) of conflict. Like other categories of nuclear weapons, its meaning is extremely problematic. For example, the Soviet Union regards Pershing II as 'strategic' because it can hit its homeland. Yet the US regards it as a 'theatre' nuclear weapon because it is intended for use in a limited nuclear war in Europe.
Tornado	An aircraft produced jointly by the UK, Italy, and West Germany. The UK is planned to have at least 385 aircraft, of which at least 220 will be the GR1 nuclear-capable variant. The total cost of the project for the UK alone is estimated to be £13,400 million at 1984 prices.
Trident C4	US SLBM which normally carries 8 warheads of 100 kilotons each. The US currently has 2304 warheads on Trident C4 missiles in service.
Trident D5	US SLBM. A completely new missile now under development capable of delivering at least 14 warheads, each rated at 300-475 kilotons. Due to be deployed from 1988 onwards, it will be the first SLBM with the ability to destroy hardened targets.
V-bombers	UK nuclear bombers first deployed in the

	1950s. Formed Britain's strategic nuclear force until Polaris came into service in 1969. Thereafter remained in a 'theatre' nuclear role until retired in 1984.
Warhead	That part of a weapon which contains the explosive, whether nuclear, chemical or conventional.
Yield	The energy released in an explosion, measured in tons of TNT, *kilotons*, or *megatons*.

Index

ABM Treaty (1972), 10-11, 21
Accidental war, 27
Air-launched ballistic missiles, 29
Alaska, 27, 82
Aldermaston, 54, 71
Andropov, Yuri, 65
Anti-ballistic missile (ABM), 10, 14, 20, 21, 22, 31, 79
Anti-submarine warfare, (ASW), 20, 22
Argentina, 68; *see also* Falklands war
Armed forces, 41, 42, 55-6, 69, 79: attitude to Trident of, 1, 58, 62
Arms talks, 3, 21, 66-7, 71; *see also* Geneva talks
Atomic bomb, development of, 4-5, 46, 68
Australia, 68

B52 bomber, 21, 27, 79
Barrow-in-Furness, 54, 58, 59
Battlefield nuclear weapons, 8, 9, 69-70, 79
Belgrano, General, 32
Bevan, Nye, 5
Blackett, Patrick, 4
Brazil, 68
Britain, 2, 23: 'Great Power' illusion in, 2, 4-5, 9, 52-3, 64
British Army, 48; *see also* Armed forces
Brown, Harold, 34

Callaghan, James, 10, 12
Campaign for Nuclear Disarmament (CND), 39
Carrington, Lord, 12
Carter, Jimmy, 12, 13
Carver, Lord, 1, 53
Chevaline, 9 *n*11, 10-11, 14, 16, 60-1, 79, 82: cost of, 10, 59, 60
China, 2, 17, 46
Christianity, 39
Churchill, Winston, 5
Cold War, 3
Conservative Party, 1, 3, 5, 9, 10, 12, 43, 58, 62, 64
Conversion (job), 62-4
Counterforce, 1, 12-13, 19, 37, 38, 39, 40, 41, 70, 79
Critchley, Julian, 39
Cruise, 1, 9, 27, 68, 69-70, 80, 84: air-launched (ALCM), 59-60, 79; as alternative to Trident, 59-61; ground-launched (GLCM), 21, 27, 43, 59, 65, 81; sea-launched (SLCM), 59, 60, 83
Cyprus, 46

Dalyell, Tam, 46-7
Decapitation strike, 25-7, 31, 51, 61, 80
Defence expenditure (UK), 1, 4, 10, 54-8, 61-2: conventional, 4, 55-6, 59, 62-4; *see also* Trident, costs of

Defence, non-nuclear, 1, 8, 48-50, 58, 61, 68-70, 71-2
Deterrent, nuclear, 1, 8, 35, 59, 71: UK independent, 9-10, 45, 47-51; *see also* Polaris; Trident
Disarmament, nuclear, 71, 72: multilateral, 3, 65-7; unilateral, 1, 5, 53, 65, 70-1

Early use, 1
Economy, UK, 62; Japanese, 62
Egypt, 68
Electromagnetic pulse, (EMP), 26, 80
Employment: alternative, 64; in defence, 61-2; in Trident production, 61-4; *see also* Conversion
Europe (as theatre of nuclear war), 8, 43, 45, 52, 69, 70; *see also* Sanctuary theory

F111 bomber, 22, 43, 69-70, 80
Failsafe/faildeadly, 28
Falklands war, 32, 46-7, 51, 64
Faslane, 31
First strike, 13, 20, 21, 22, 23-5, 27, 30, 31, 35, 43, 49, 50, 59, 60, 80; *see also* Decapitation strike
First use, 2, 8, 42, 50, 69; *see also* No first use
Flexible response, 5, 39, 70, 80
France, 2, 9, 23, 29, 37, 43, 48, 52-3, 65, 66-7, 68
Freeze: superpower, 70-1; US, 69

GCHQ Cheltenham, 33
Geneva talks, 26-7, 65-6
Global Strategy Paper, 5
Greece, 68
Green parties, 69
Greenham Common, 29, 43, 59, 65, 81

Harrier GR5, 9
Healey, Denis, 12
Heath, Edward, 10
Heseltine, Michael, 61
Hill-Norton, Lord, 53
Hiroshima, 39, 81
Holland, 69
Holy Loch, 29, 43
Howe, Geoffrey, 12

India, 18, 46, 68
Indian Ocean, 23
Indonesia, 46
Intercontinental ballistic missile (ICBM), 13, 24-5, 35, 81
Intermediate nuclear forces (INF), 26-7, 65-6, 81
Iran, 68
Iraq, 3, 68
Israel, 3, 67, 68

Italy, 68, 84

Japan, 18, 52, 68
Just war doctrine, 39

Kings Bay, Georgia, 29
Kinnock, Neil, 1

Labour Party, 1, 3, 9-10, 11, 12, 61
Lakenheath, 43, 80
Launch-on-warning, 26-8, 81
Liberal Party, 1, 69
Libya, 68
Limited nuclear options policy, 37, 40
Limited nuclear war, 20, 24, 38, 43-5, 80

MX missile, 22, 27, 30, 35, 81
Macmillan, Harold, 5, 9
Minuteman, 22, 82
Molesworth, 29, 81
Mondale, Walter, 70
Moscow criterion, 10, 11
Mulley, Fred, 12
Multiple independently targetable re-entry vehicles (MIRV), 13, 21, 22, 25, 38, 66, 81, 83
Multiple re-entry vehicles (MRV), 16, 81, 82, 83

Nassau agreement (1962), 9
Navsat, 32
Navstar Global Positioning System, 32
Nixon, Richard, 47, 50
No first use, 8, 69-70, 82
Non-Proliferation Treaty, 1968 (NPT), 67, 68
North Atlantic Treaty Organisation (NATO), 5, 8, 10, 24, 30, 35-6, 38, 39, 41-2, 43, 45, 46, 53, 56, 58, 66, 68, 69, 70, 72, 80, 81, 82
Nott, John, 16-17, 49
Nuclear umbrella, 41, 46
Nuclear warfighting, 3, 20, 25, 35, 36, 37, 40
Nuclear-weapon-free zone, 69-70, 71
Nuclear winter, 52, 82

Omaha, 36
Overkill, 40, 66
Owen, David, 12, 59

Pakistan, 3, 67, 68
Peace movements, 1, 39, 68
Pershing II, 27, 30, 60, 61, 68, 69-70, 82, 84
Plutonium, 29
Polaris, 1, 9-10, 11, 43, 65, 82: capability of, 9, 11, 16, 17, 21, 23, 27, 35, 39, 47, 60-1, 66, 67; cost of, 10 *n*13, 54, 55, 59; development of, 5, 9, 10, 29, 31, 59, 79, 85; Trident as a replacement for, 2, 9, 12, 13, 16, 20, 21, 72; *see also* Chevaline
Portugal, 68

Poseidon, 27, 29, 43, 82
Potsdam, 4
Pre-emptive strike, 35, 50, 59
Pre-delegation, 23, 27, 82
Pressurised water reactor mark II (PWRII), 13, 16
Proliferation, 46, 50, 67-8; *see also* Non-Proliferation Treaty
Public opinion, 1 *n*1
Pym, Francis, 12

Reagan, Ronald, 13, 16, 20, 22, 24, 25, 81
Retaliatory strikes, 5, 38, 50, 51, 52
Rodgers, William, 1
Royal Air Force, 9, 48, 59-60; *see also* Armed Forces
Royal Navy, 43, 59, 62-4; *see also* Armed forces

SS20, 25, 65, 83
Sanctuary theory, 40, 42-5, 51
Sandys, Duncan, 46
Second centre theory, 40, 41-2, 45, 51
Single Integrated Operational Plan (SIOP), 30, 40, 83
Skybolt, 29
Skynet, 32, 54
Social Democratic Party (SDP), 1
Socialism, 68-9; *see also* Labour Party
South Africa, 67, 68
South Korea, 18, 67, 68
Soviet Union, 2, 9, 10, 13, 22, 65: as a target, 18, 21, 23, 24, 25, 26-7, 33, 35, 38-9, 41-2, 50, 51, 59; conventional attack by, 8, 40, 41, 42, 45, 48-9, 51, 69; nuclear attack by, 20, 21, 22, 23, 24-5, 26, 31, 37, 38, 43-5; *see also* Moscow criterion
Spain, 68
Speed, Keith, 47, 59
Star wars, 22
Strategic arms limitation talks (SALT), 65, 66-7, 83; SALT II, 16, 66-7, 84
Strategic arms reduction talks (START), 25, 66, 84
Strategic nuclear weapons, 5, 9-11, 12, 13, 55, 60, 65, 67, 69, 84
Submarine-launched ballistic missile (SLBM), 13, 22, 82
Supreme Allied Commander, Europe (SACEUR, NATO), 30
Sweden, 50

Tactical nuclear weapons, 5, 8, 13, 47, 48, 55, 60, 69, 84
Taiwan, 67
Thatcher, Margaret, 1, 10, 12, 16, 30, 64
Theatre nuclear weapons, 5-9, 41, 43, 45, 55, 59, 60, 66, 69-70, 81, 84, 85
Third world, 3, 45-7; *see also* Non-Proliferation Treaty
Tizard, Henry, 4
Tomahawk missile, 59

Tories, *see* Conservative Party

Tornado, 9, 22, 41, 59, 69-70, 84

Trident C4, 12, 13, 16, 27, 36, 37, 40, 54, 60, 66, 84

Trident D5, 13, 16-17, 20, 23, 27, 30, 35, 36, 37, 54, 60, 61, 65, 66, 70, 71, 84

Trident, accuracy of, 20, 23-4, 25, 36, 37, 38, 39; availability of, 17, 20, 21, 22, 23; as escalation factor, 1, 2, 12, 13-14, 16-21, 67; cancellation of, 3; communications with, 30, 31-2, 33, 54; cost of, 1, 12, 13, 15, 23, 40, 42, 54-64, 71, 72; cost of (production), 54, 56 *n*9; cost of (operational), 54-5; deterrence value of, 21, 22, 35, 36, 40-1, 45, 47-8, 9-50, 51, 66, 67, 72; independence of, 8-34, 68; independence of (construction), 8-30, 58, 62; independence of (operational), 1, 25, 26, 30-4, 40, 51; navigation of, 32; nuclear alternatives to, 39, 58-61; range of, 18, 19, 21, 22, 23, 27; retaliation by, 22-3, 25; survivability f, 21, 22-3; targeting of, 17-19, 20, 25, 26, 30-1, 32, 33, 35-41; targeting (hard), 20, 21, 24, 27, 31, 35, 36-7, 38, 81, 84; testing of, 29; warheads on, 16-17, 20, 21, 24, 25, 26, 27, 28, 38, 66; *see also* Conversion; Defence spending; Employment

Trigger theory, 51-2

Turkey, 68

UN Security Council, 2